RYAN ADAMS

ROCK N ROLL

GUITAR
TAB
EDITION

D1591723

Wise Publications
part of The Music Sales Group

London / New York / Paris / Sydney / Copenhagen / Berlin / Madrid / Tokyo

Published by:
Wise Publications,
8/9 Frith Street, London W1D 3JB, England.

Exclusive distributors:

Music Sales Limited,
Distribution Centre, Newmarket Road, Bury St. Edmunds,
Suffolk IP33 3YB, England.

Music Sales Corporation,
257 Park Avenue South, New York,
NY10010, United States of America.

Music Sales Pty Limited
120 Rothschild Avenue, Rosebery,
NSW 2018, Australia.

Order No. AM979671
ISBN 1-84449-406-3
This book © Copyright 2004 by Wise Publications.

Music arrangements by Jon Paxman/Martin Shellard.
Music processed by Paul Ewers Music Design/Jon Paxman.

Printed in the United Kingdom by
Printwise (Haverhill) Limited, Suffolk.

www.musicsales.com

THIS IS IT

Words & Music by Ryan Adams and Johnny T. Yerington

Chorus

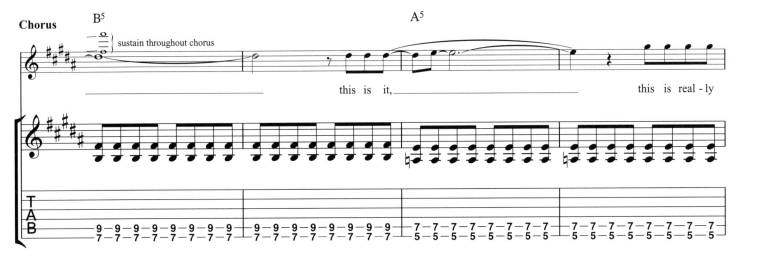

this is it,_____ this is real - ly

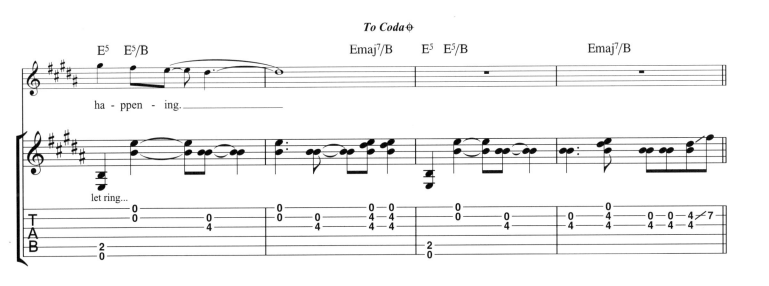

ha - ppen - ing._____

let ring...

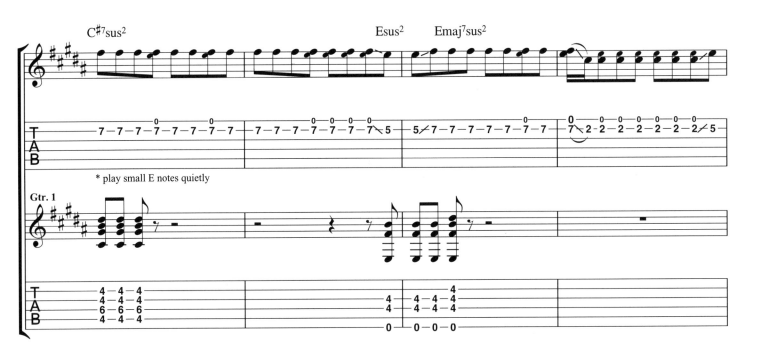

* play small E notes quietly

8

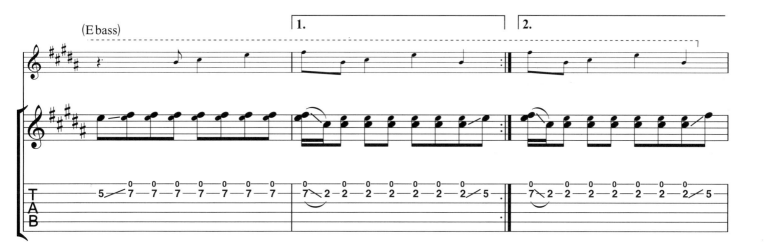

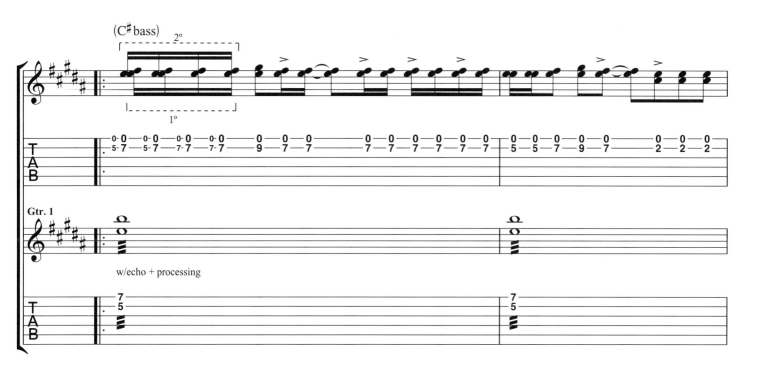

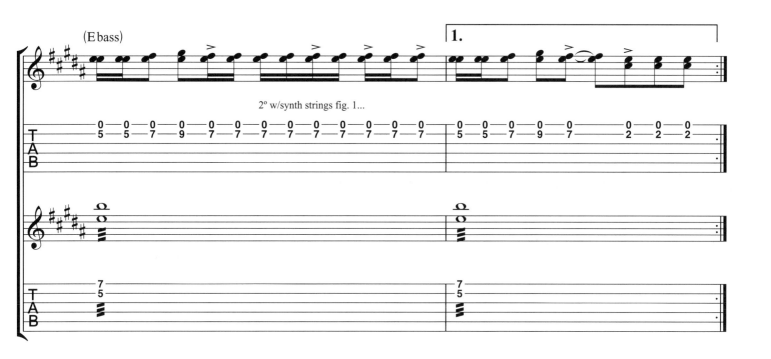

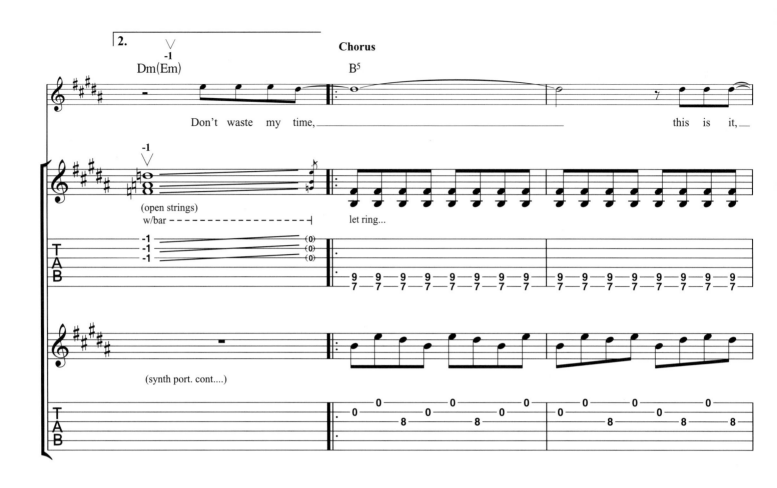

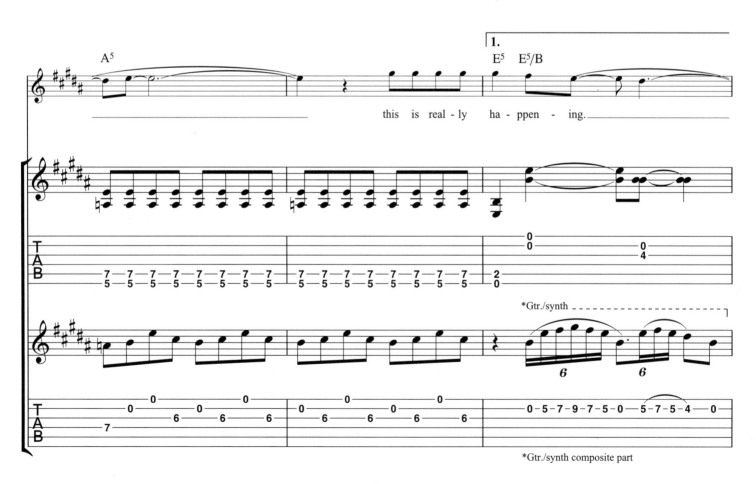

*Gtr./synth composite part

SHALLOW

Words & Music by Ryan Adams

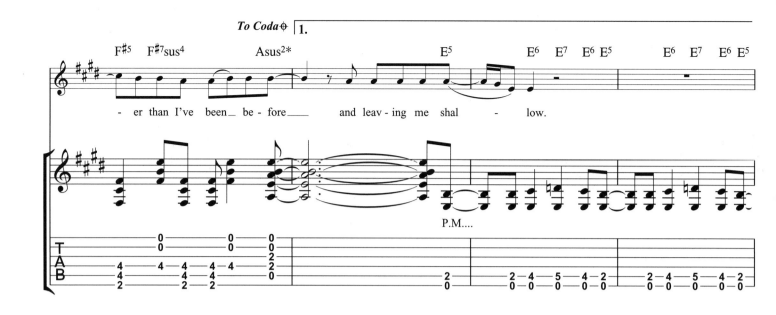

-er than I've been_ be-fore___ and leav-ing me shal - low.

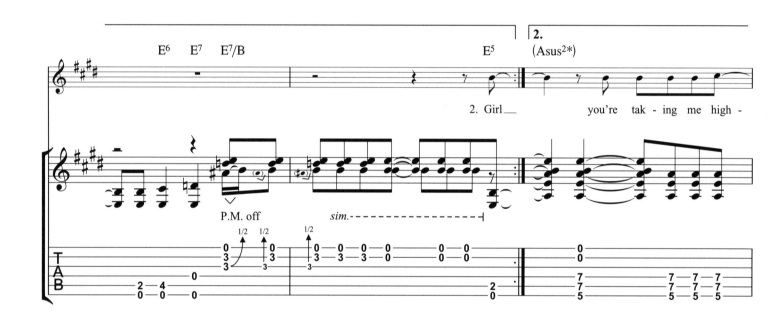

2. Girl__ you're tak - ing me high-

-er,___ you're tak - ing me high - er.___

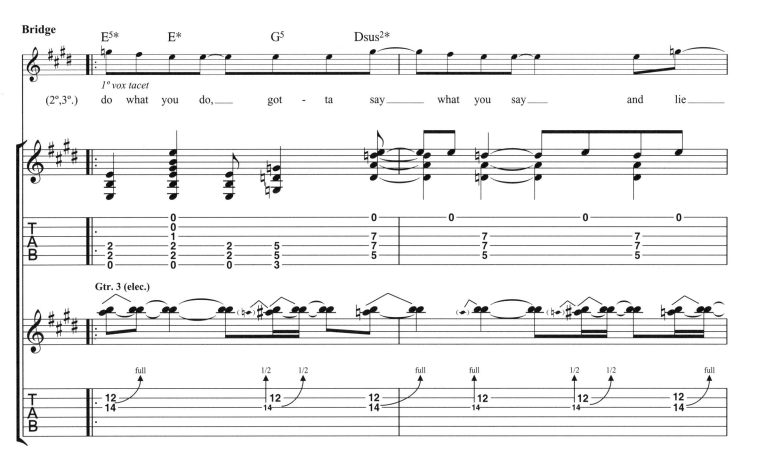

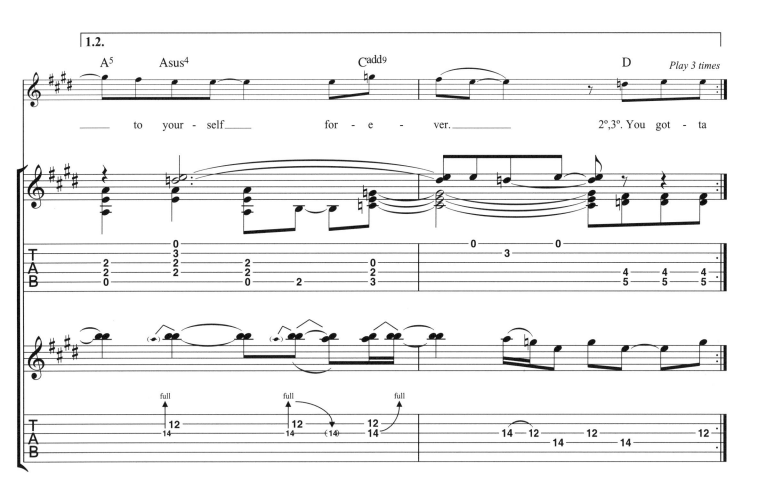

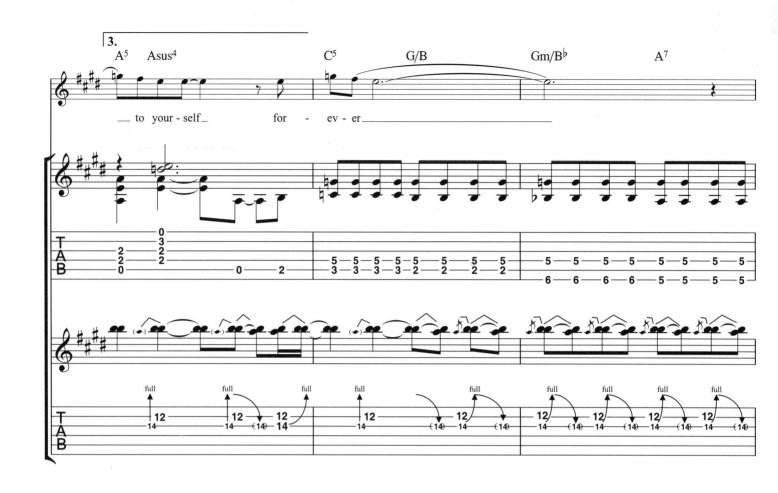

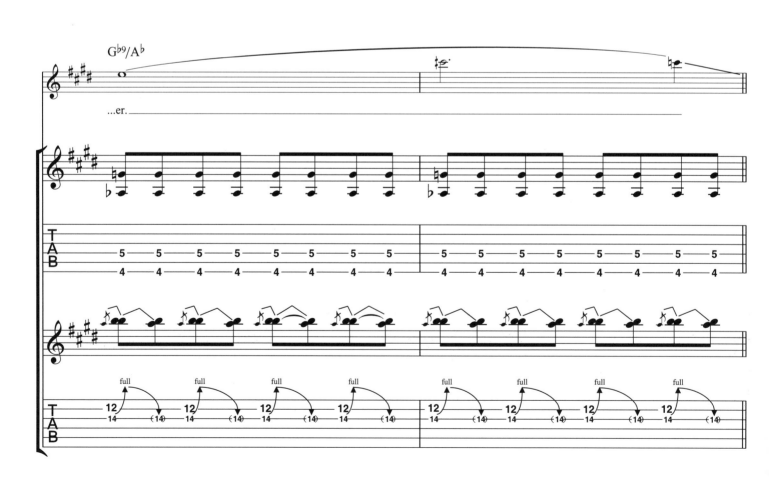

16

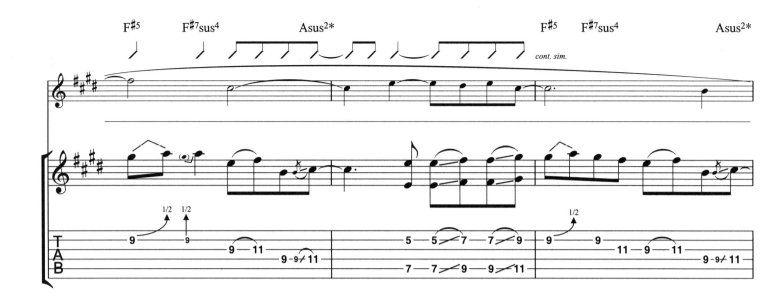

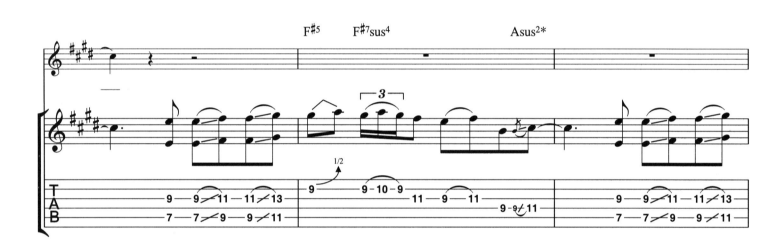

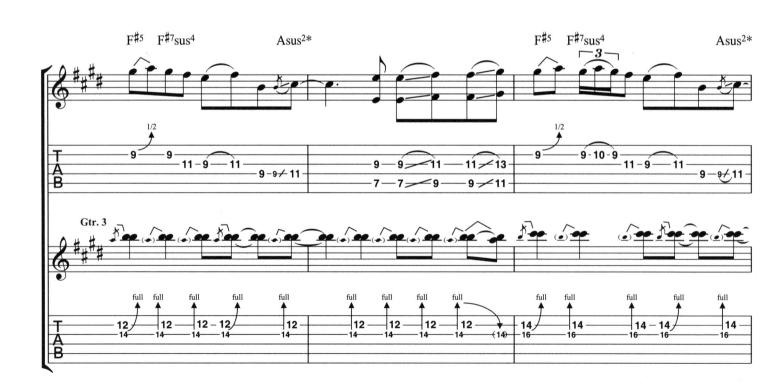

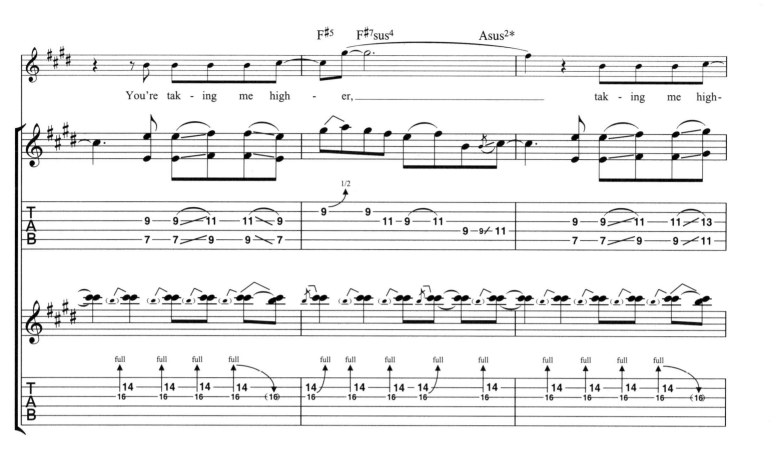

You're tak - ing me high - er,_____ tak - ing me high-

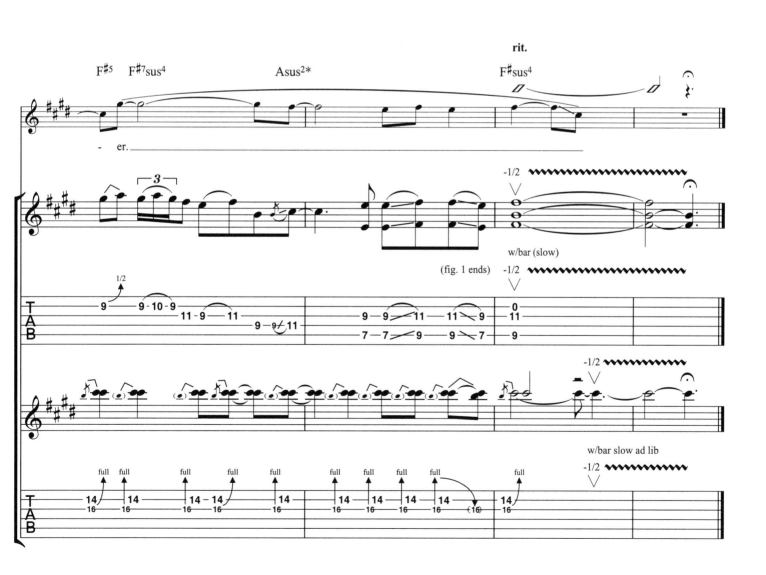

- er._____

1974

Words & Music by Ryan Adams

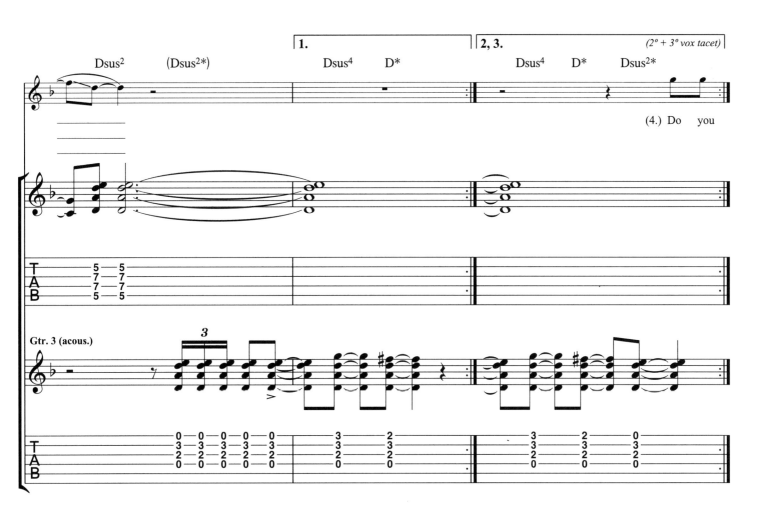

Instrumental/chorus

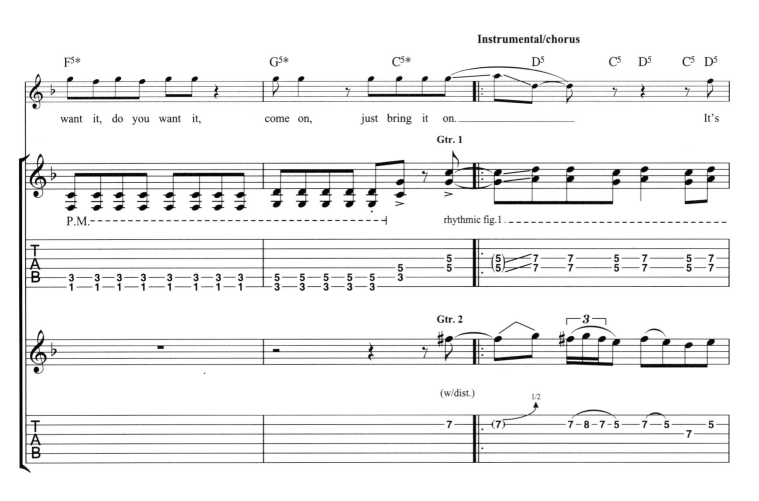

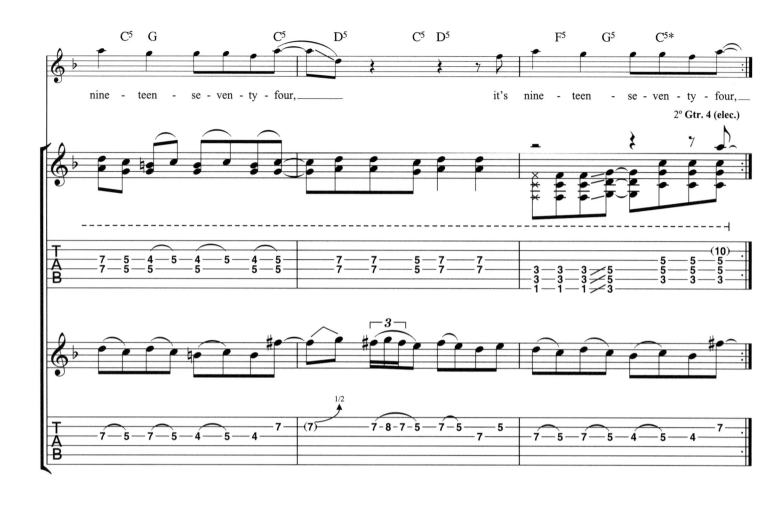

nine - teen - se - ven - ty - four,_____ it's nine - teen - se - ven - ty - four,__

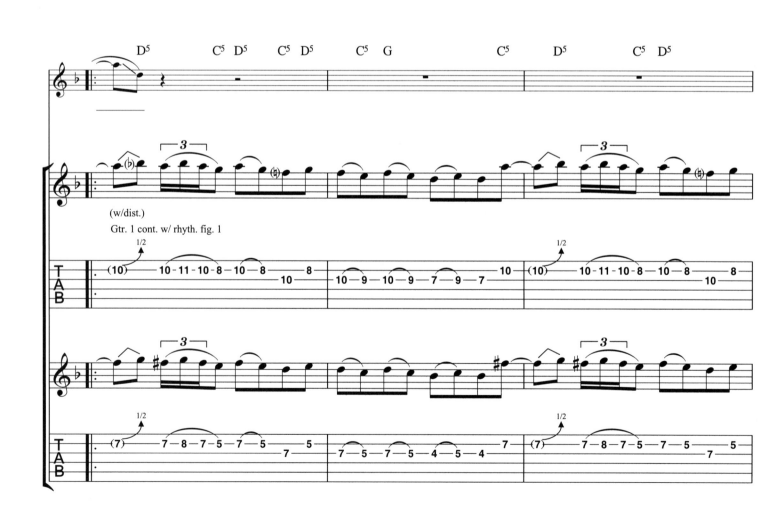

SO ALIVE

Words & Music by Ryan Adams and Johnny T. Yerington

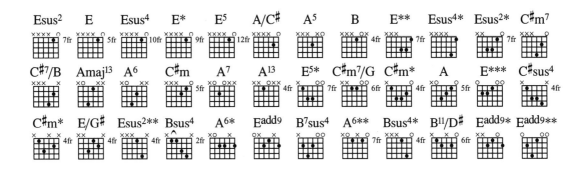

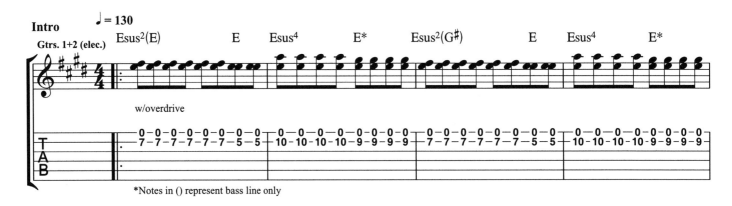

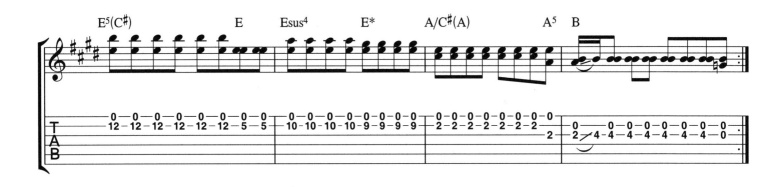

*Notes in () represent bass line only

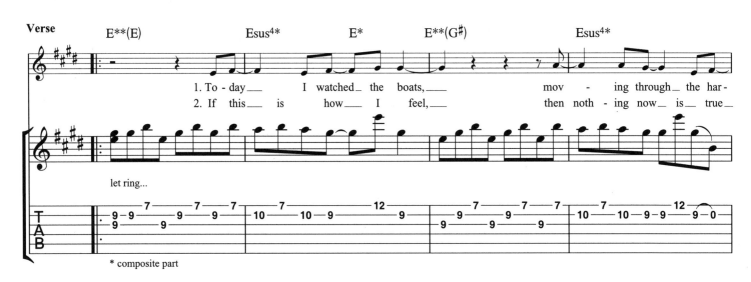

* composite part

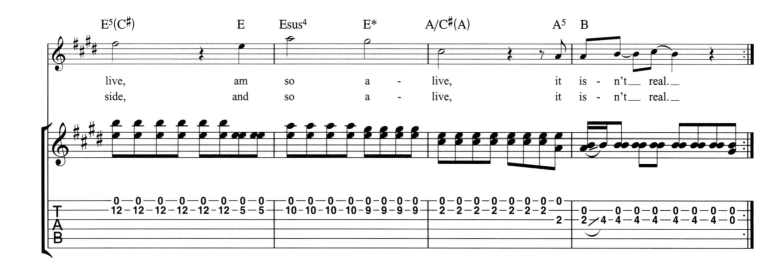

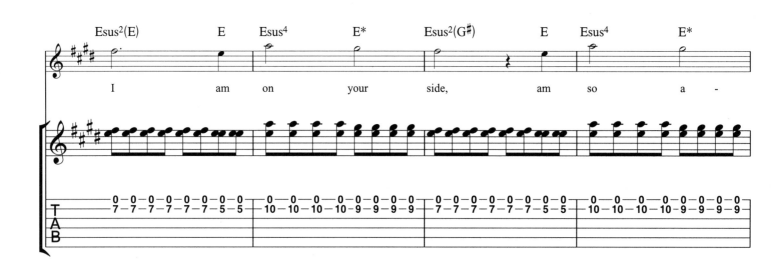

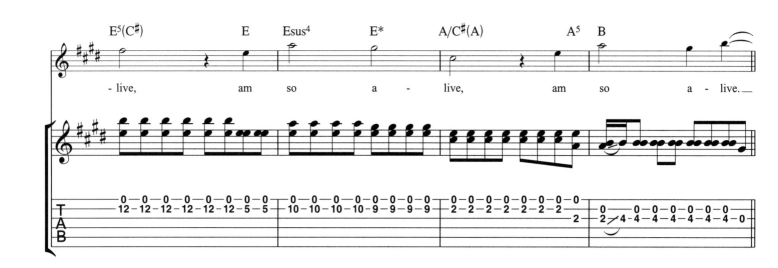

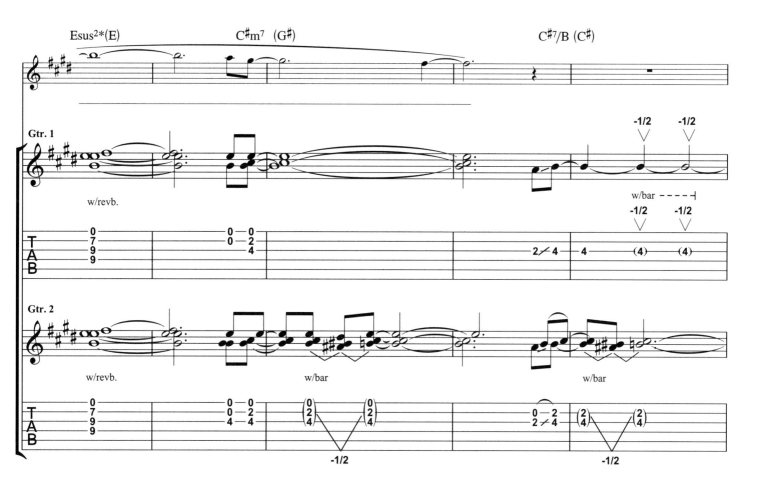

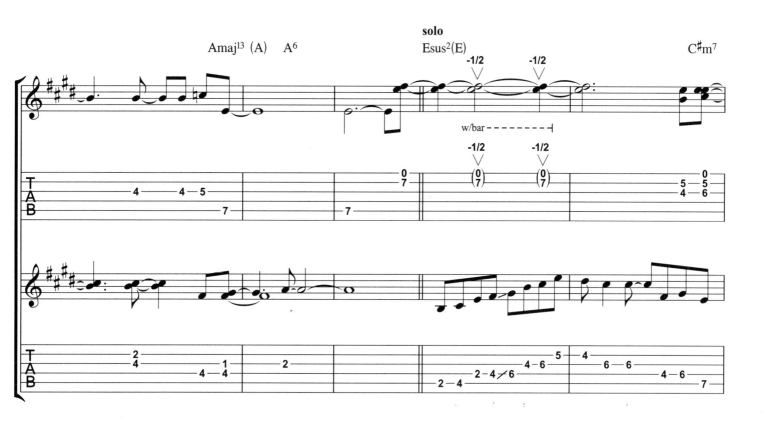

30

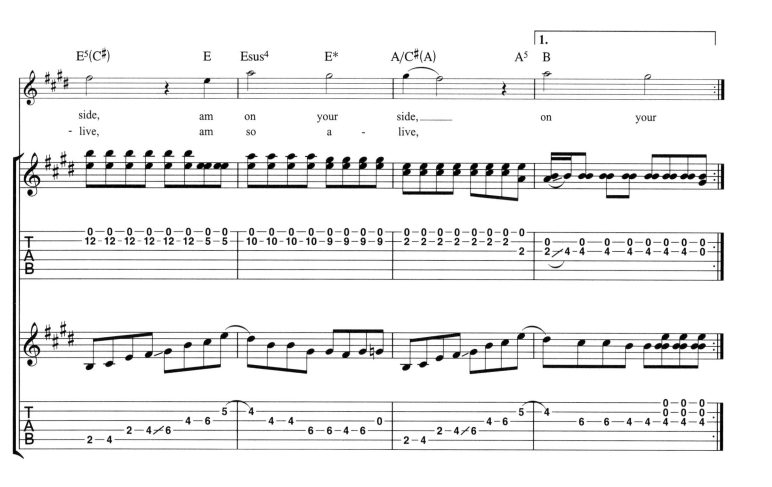

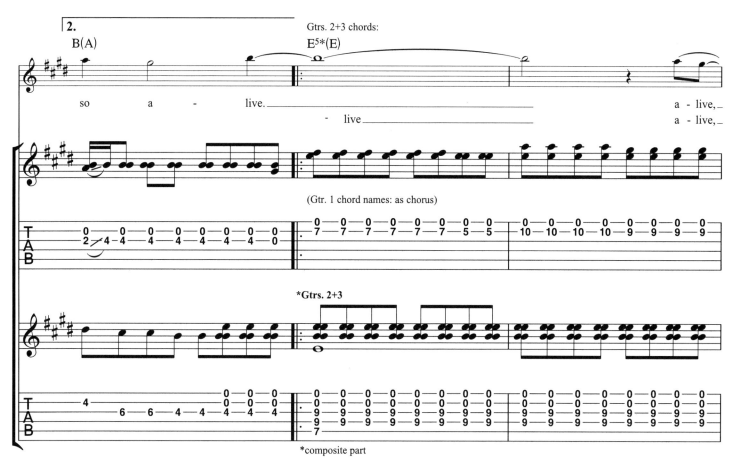

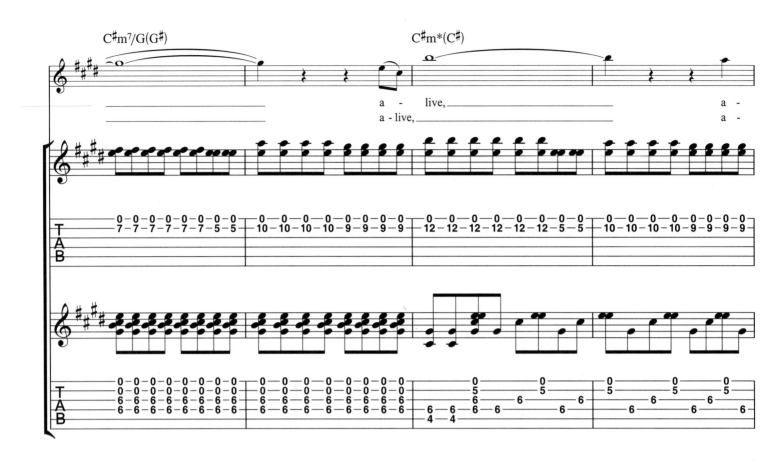

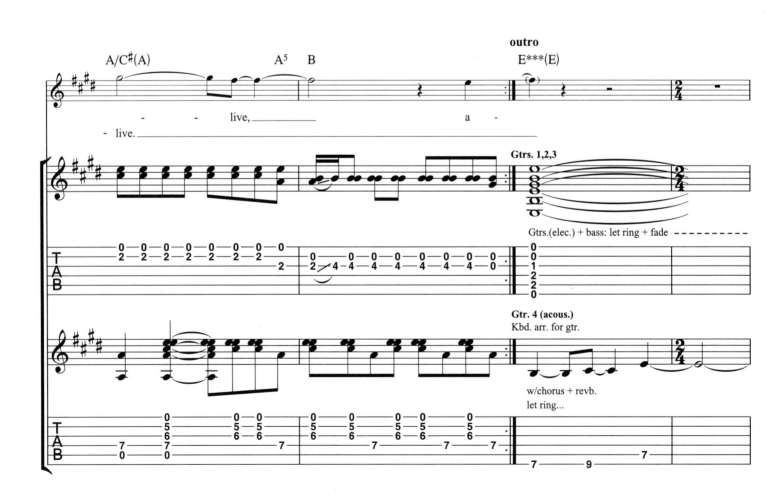

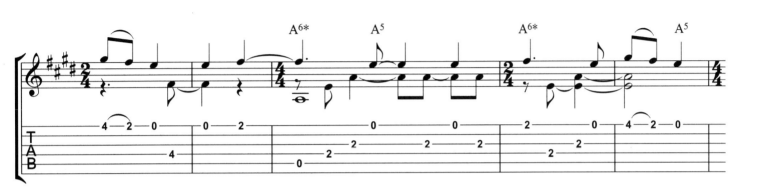

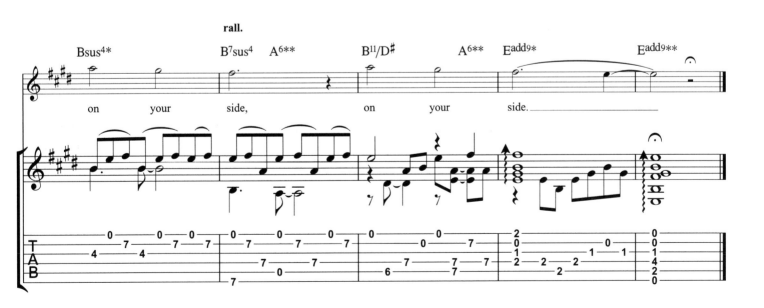

LUMINOL

Words & Music by Ryan Adams, Johnny T. Yerington and Tony Shanahan

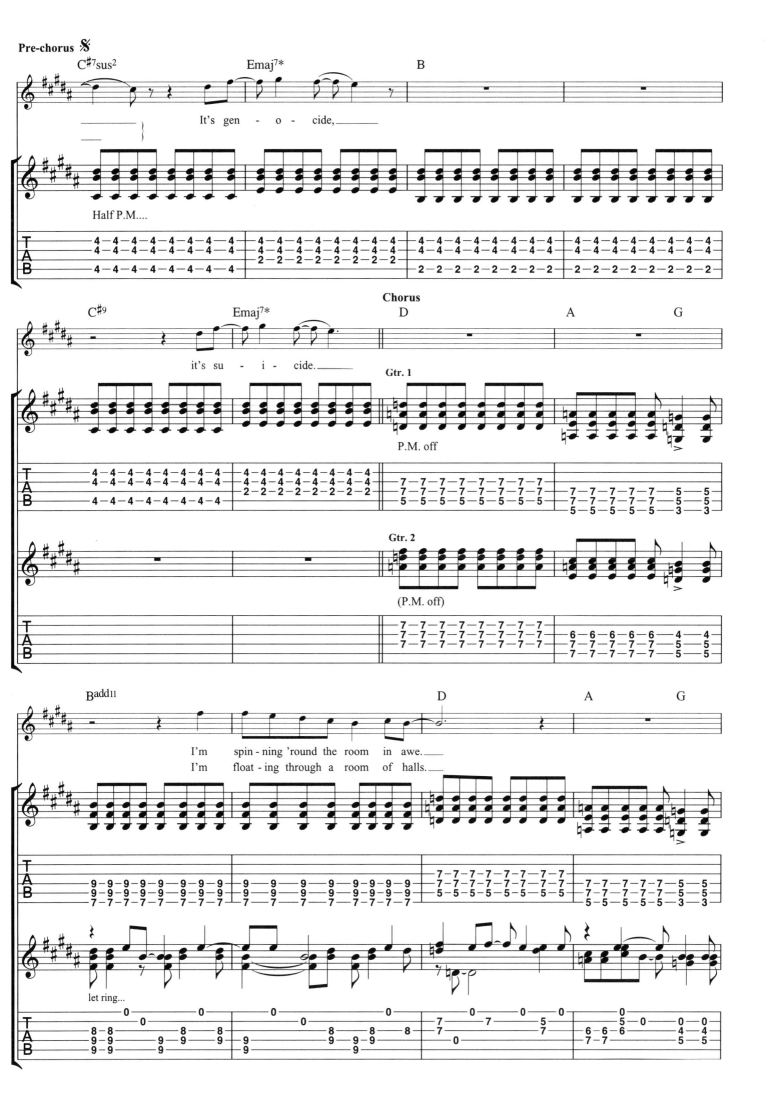

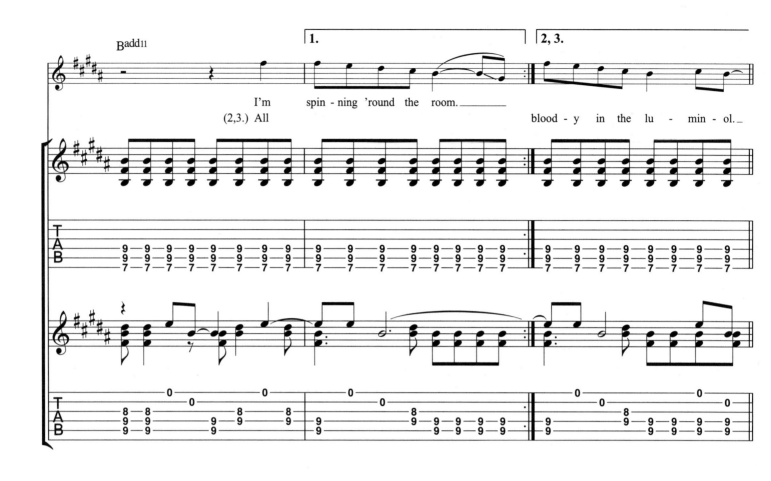

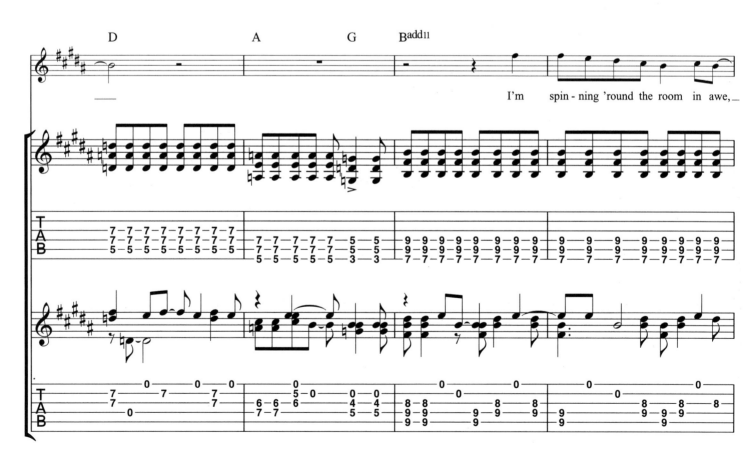

36

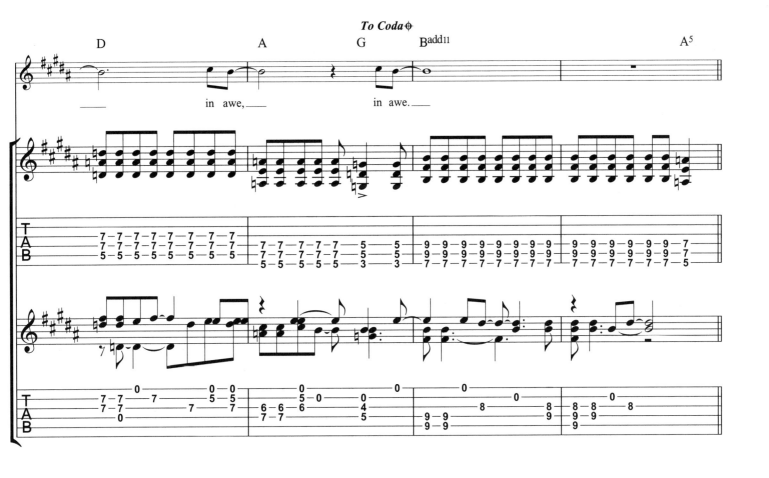

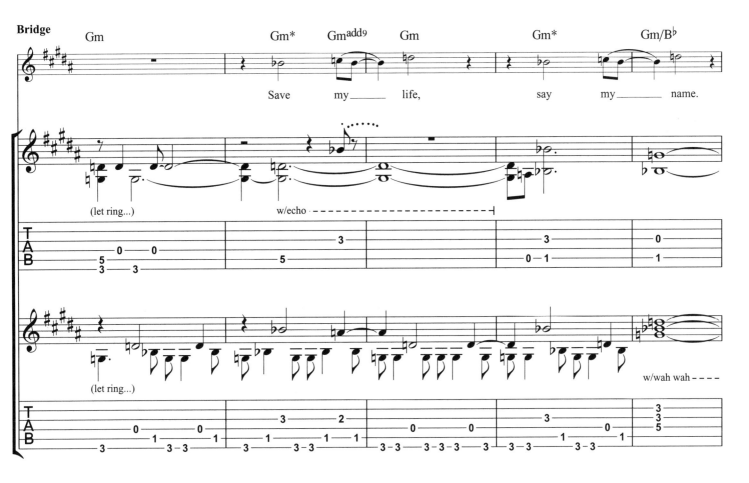

Save my ___ life, say my ___

w/moderate echo

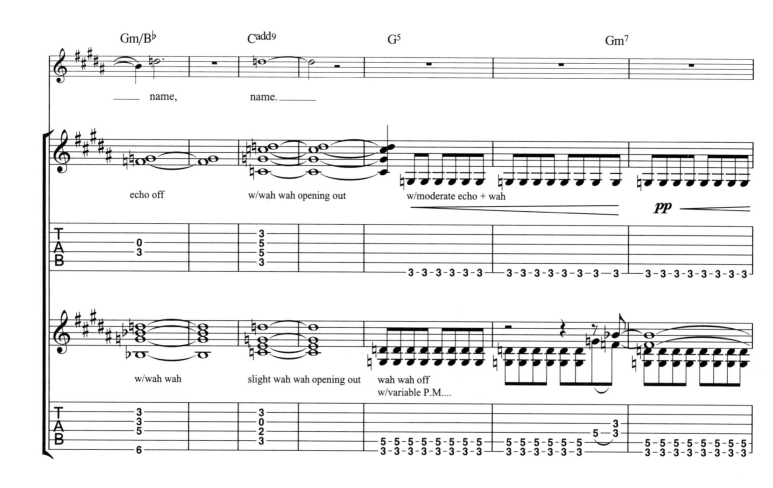

name, name. ___

echo off

w/wah wah opening out

w/moderate echo + wah

pp

w/wah wah

slight wah wah opening out

wah wah off
w/variable P.M....

39

BURNING PHOTOGRAPHS

Words & Music by Ryan Adams and Johnny T. Yerington

Verse

-ally see___ the light,___ down on the east___ side,___ wast - ed like a mem - o - ry. If I had___
-fic sings___ the songs,___ in - vit - ing me in___ to dodge the bul - lets from an emp - ty gun. If I had___

___ a car___ I'd drive_____ straight off the bridge___ in - to the riv - er, it would emp - ty me.
___ a car___ I'd drive_____ straight in - to the win - dow of a bank I owed mon - ey to.

Pre-chorus 𝄋

Pre - tty pic - tures in a mag - a - zine,___ ev - ery - bo - dy is so make - be - lieve___ it's true.___

Gtr. 2

let ring...

2, 3.

-graphs._____ You're doomed to re-peat____ the past,____ 'cause no-thing is gon-

To Coda

-na last,_____ I burned all your pho-to - graphs._____ And

(%)_____

Bridge

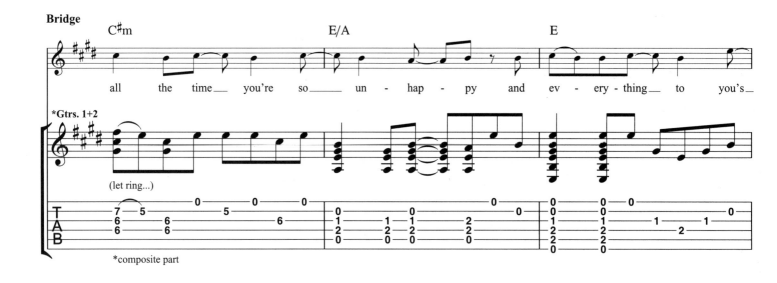

all the time___ you're so___ un - hap - py and ev - ery - thing___ to you's___

(let ring...)

*composite part

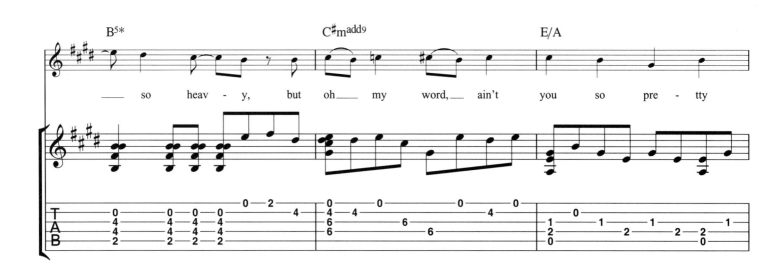

___ so heav - y, but oh___ my word,___ ain't you so pre - tty

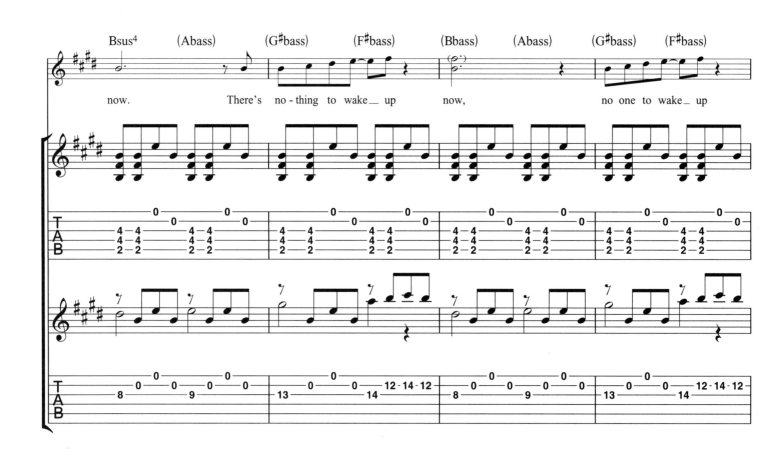

now. There's no - thing to wake___ up now, no one to wake___ up

SHE'S LOST TOTAL CONTROL

Words & Music by Ryan Adams

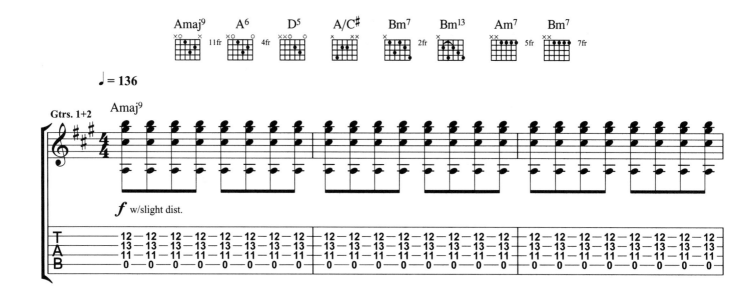

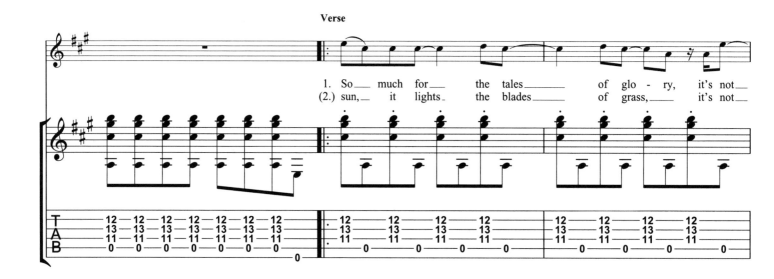

1. So much for the tales of glo - ry, it's not
(2.) sun, it lights the blades of grass, it's not

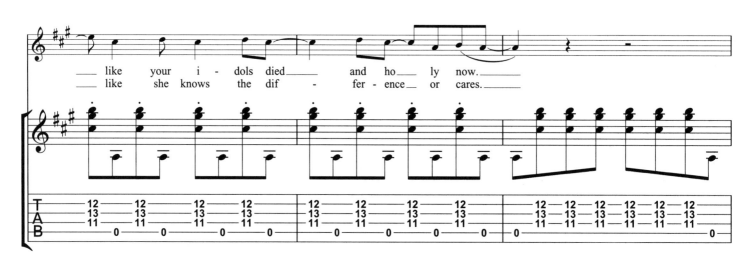

___ like your i - dols died and ho - ly now.
___ like she knows the dif - fer - ence or cares.

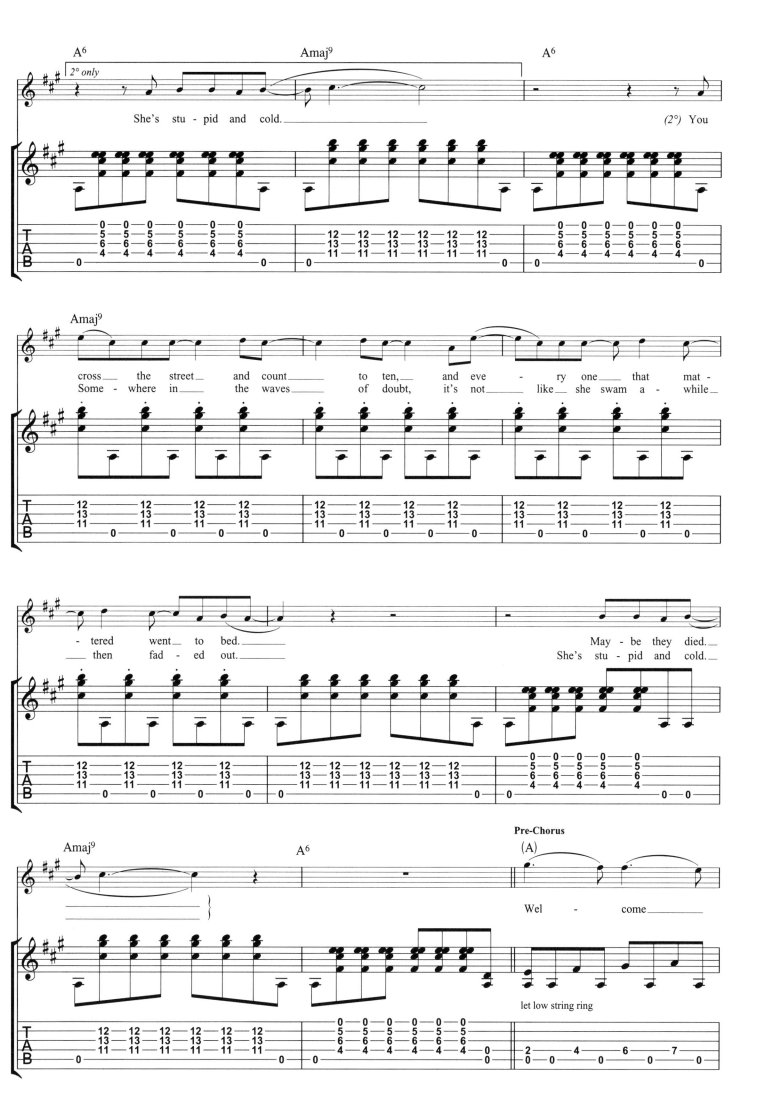

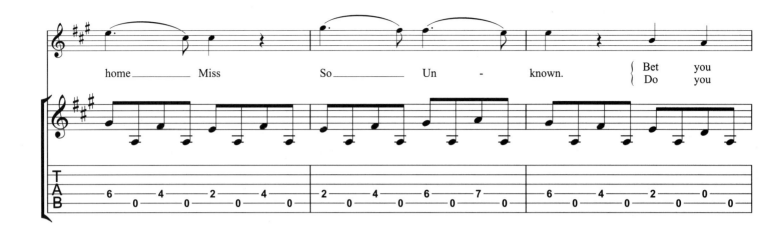

home_____ Miss So_____ Un - known. {Bet you / Do you}

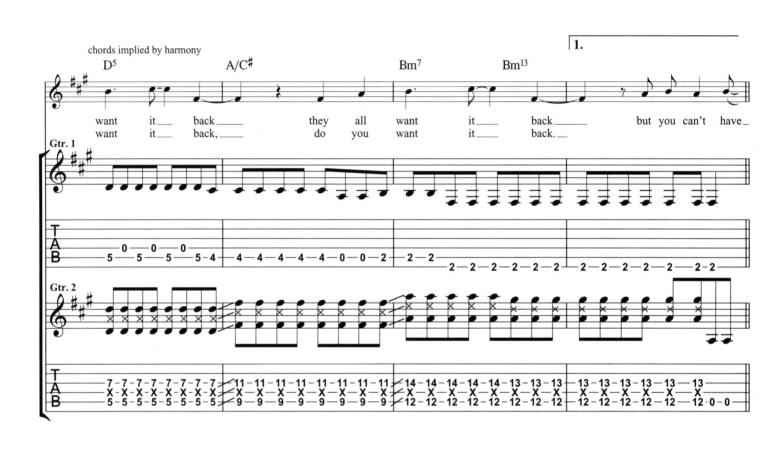

chords implied by harmony

D5   A/C#   Bm7   Bm13   **1.**

want it____ back_____   they all want it____ back_____   but you can't have__
want it____ back,____   do you want it____ back.__

Gtr. 1

Gtr. 2

Chorus

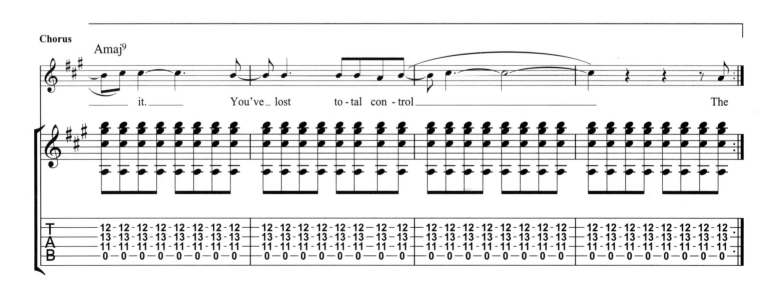

Amaj9

____ it.____ You've_ lost to - tal con - trol_____ The

48

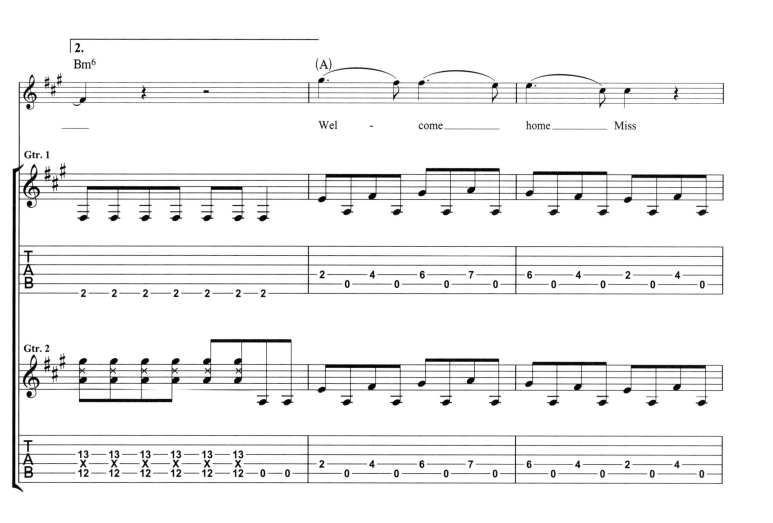

Wel - come _____ home _____ Miss

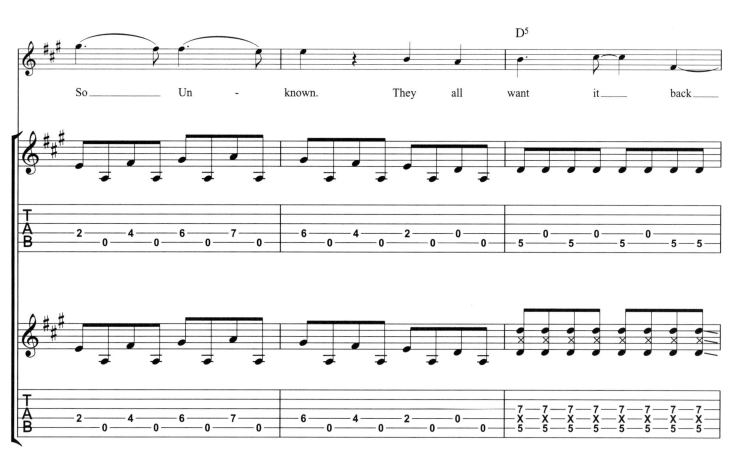

So _____ Un - known. They all want it _____ back _____

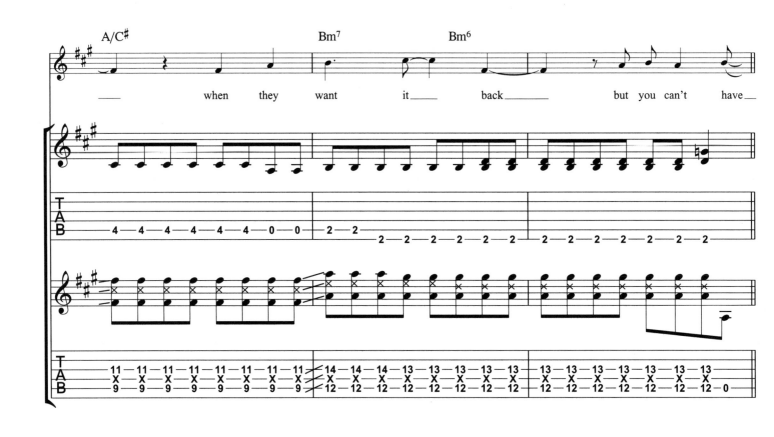

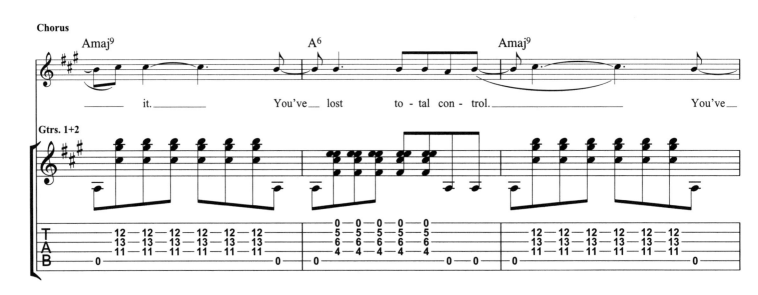

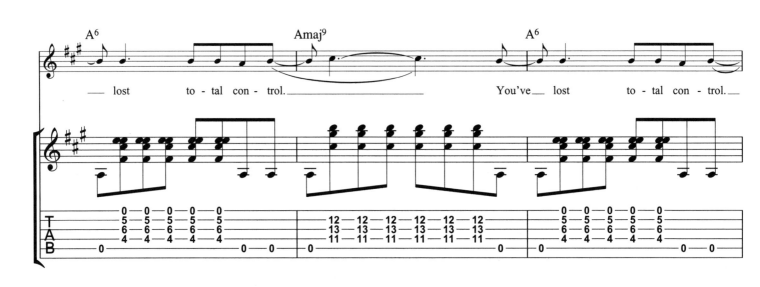

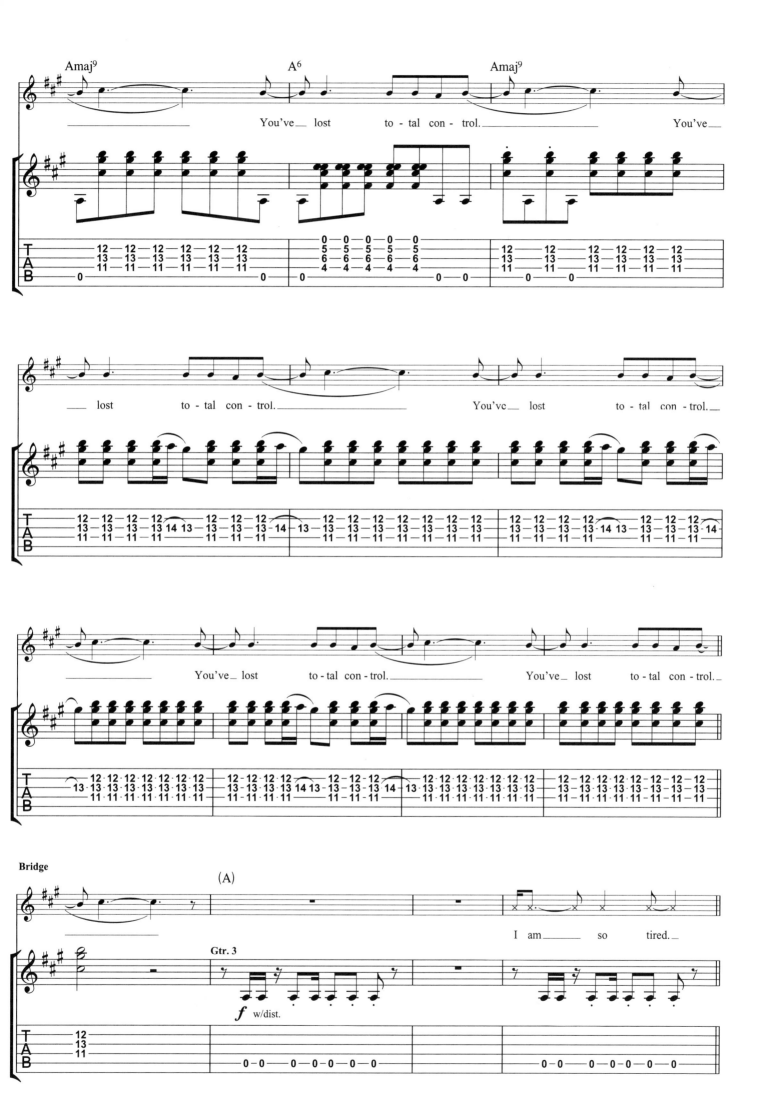

I am so, I am so,

I am so, I am so,

I am so, I am so, I am so, I am so,

I am so, I am so, I am so, tired.

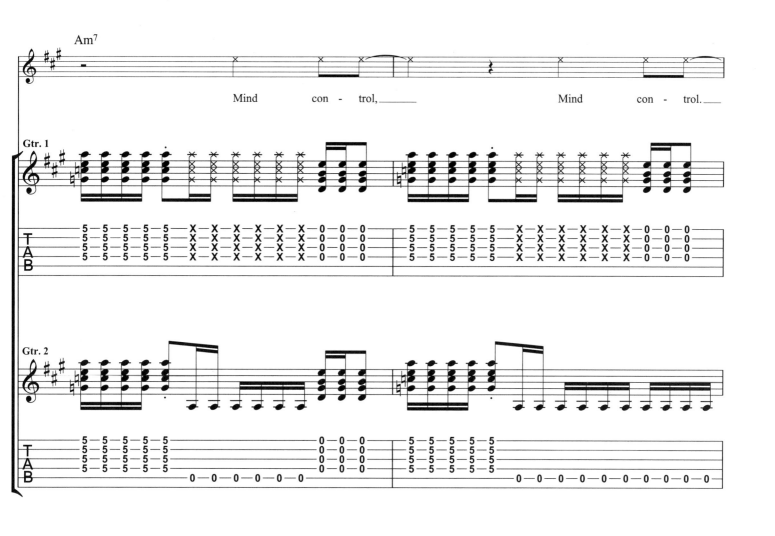

Mind con - trol,_____ Mind con - trol.____

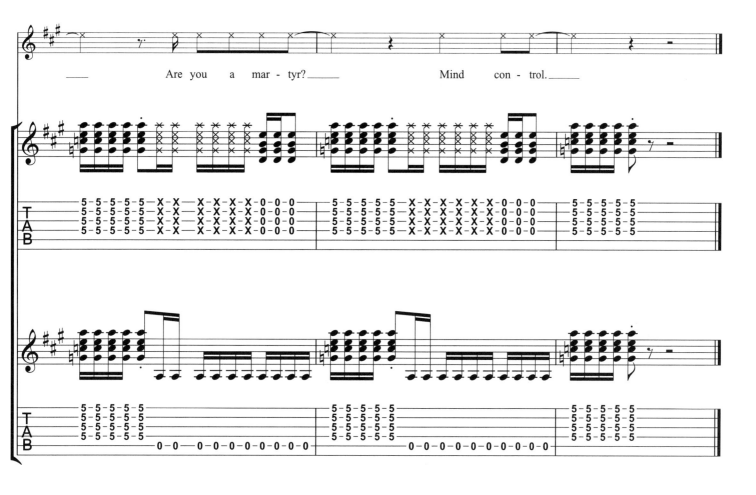

____ Are you a mar - tyr?_____ Mind con - trol._____

NOTE TO SELF: DON'T DIE

Words & Music by Ryan Adams and Parker Posey

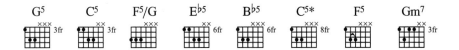

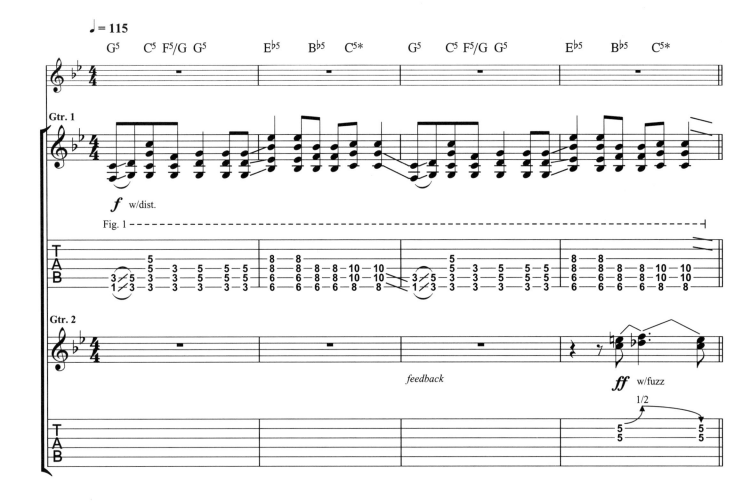

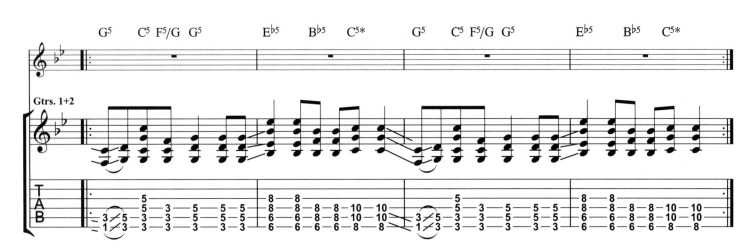

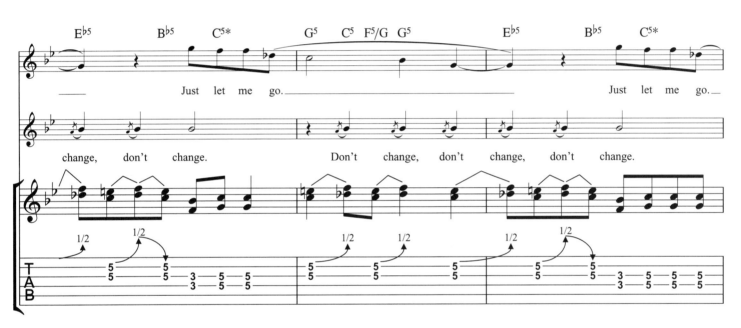

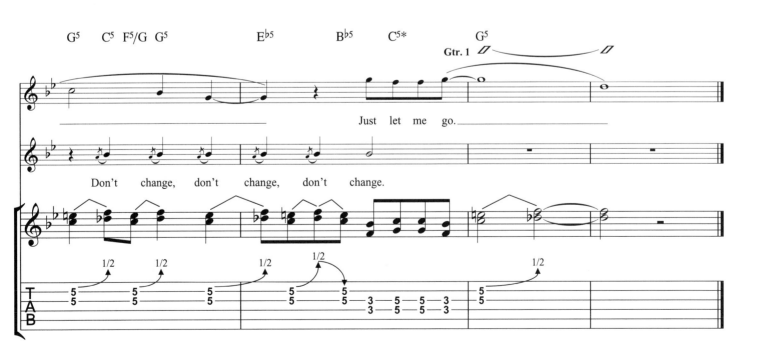

57

WISH YOU WERE HERE

Words & Music by Ryan Adams and Brad Rice

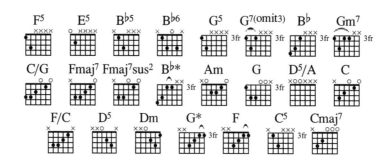

* Symbols in () represent Gtr. 3 (acous.) chords

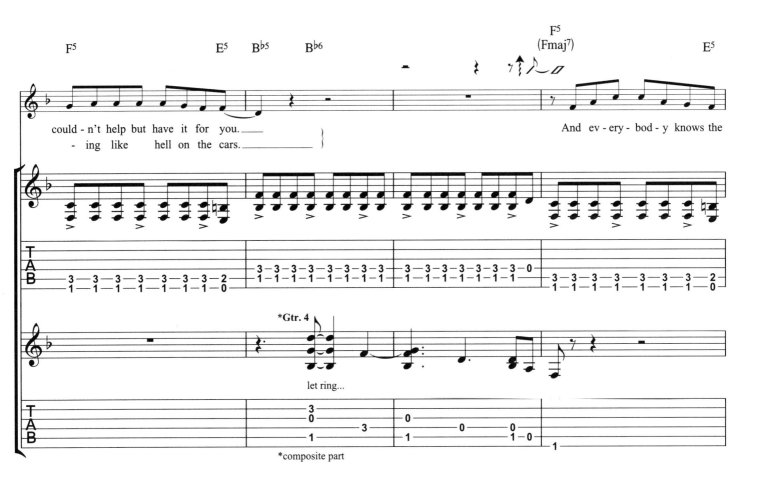

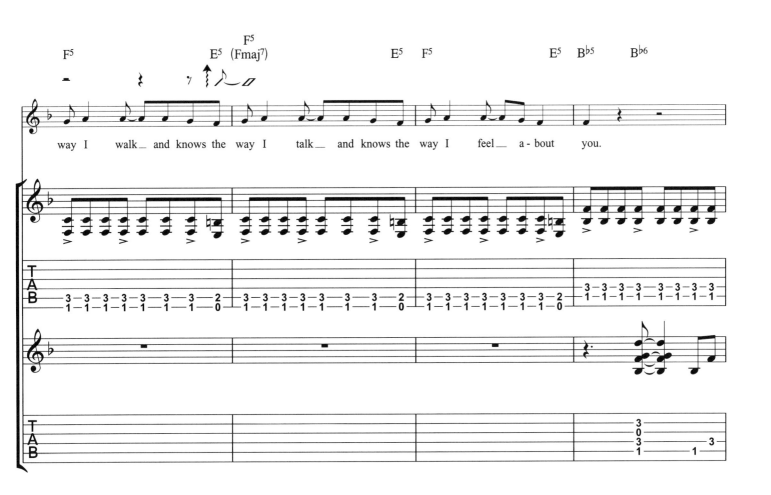

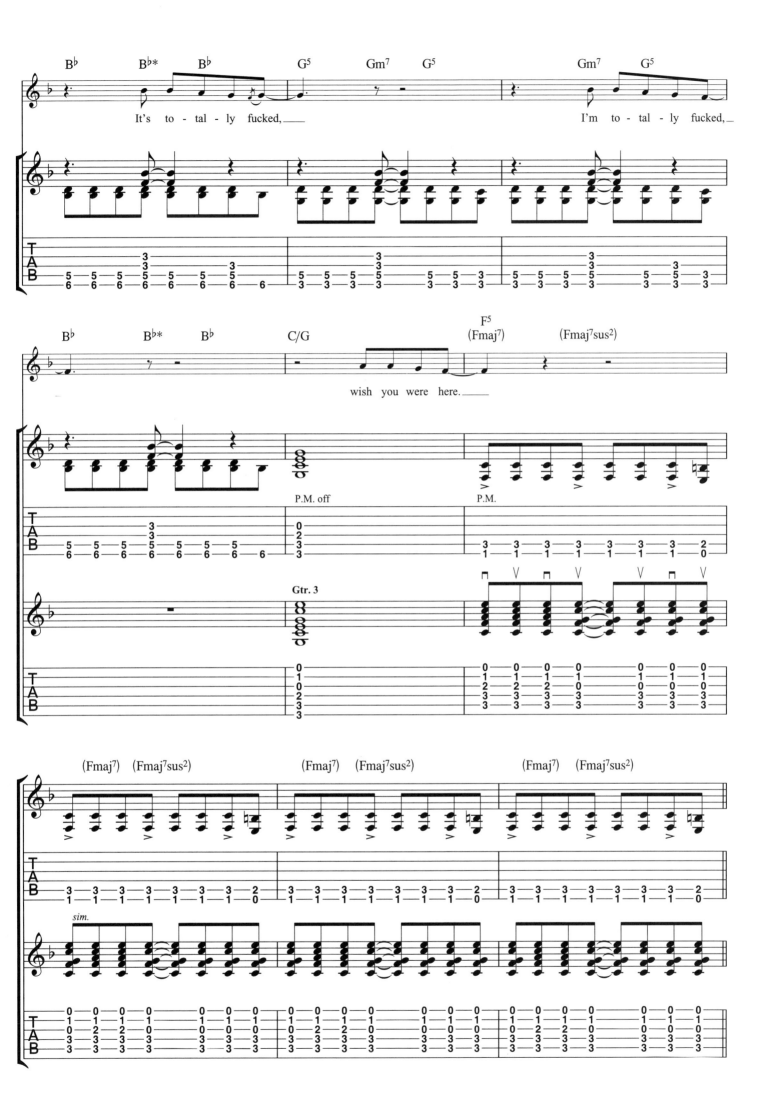

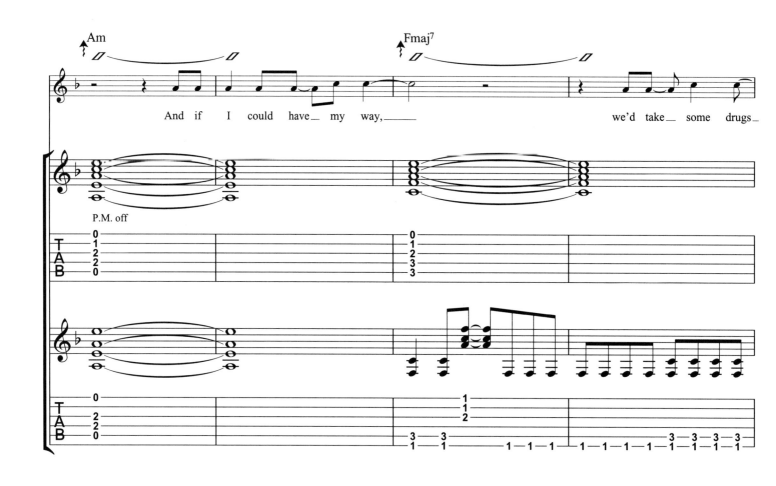

And if I could have_ my way,_____ we'd take_ some drugs_

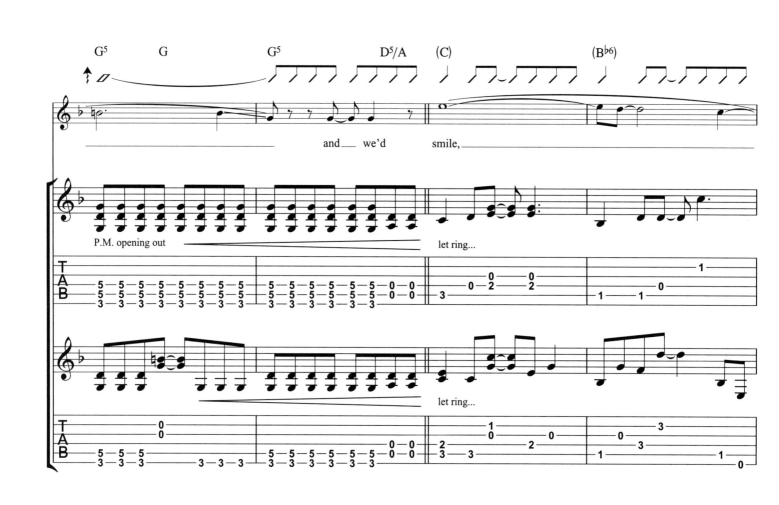

and_ we'd smile,_____

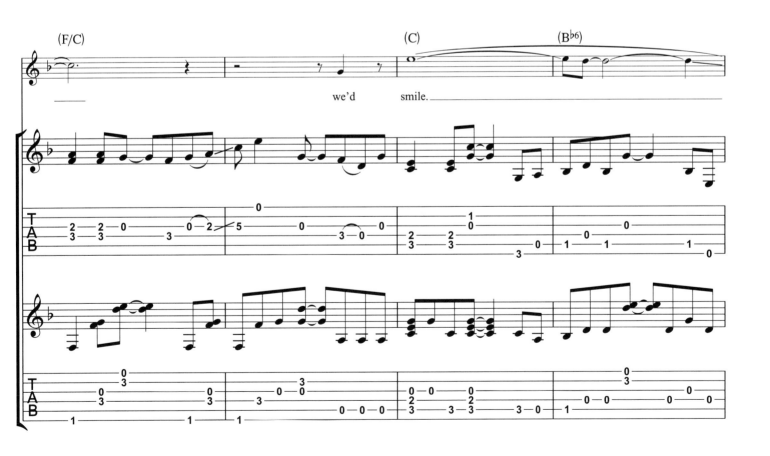

But not to-night_____ my

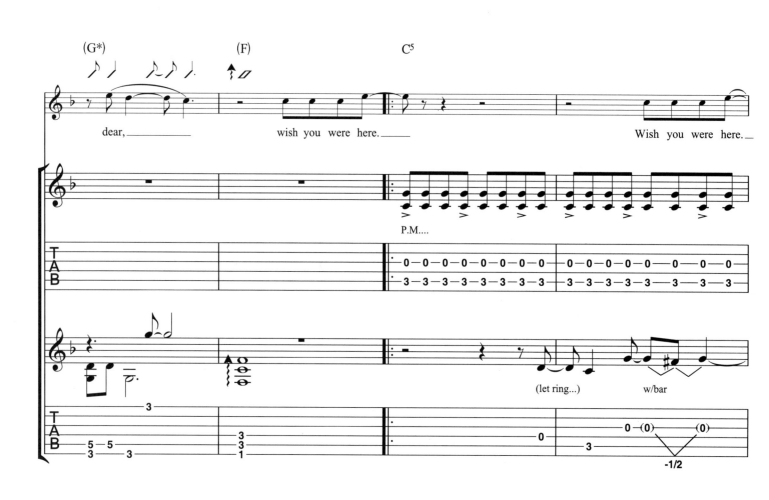

dear,_____ wish you were here._____ Wish you were here._

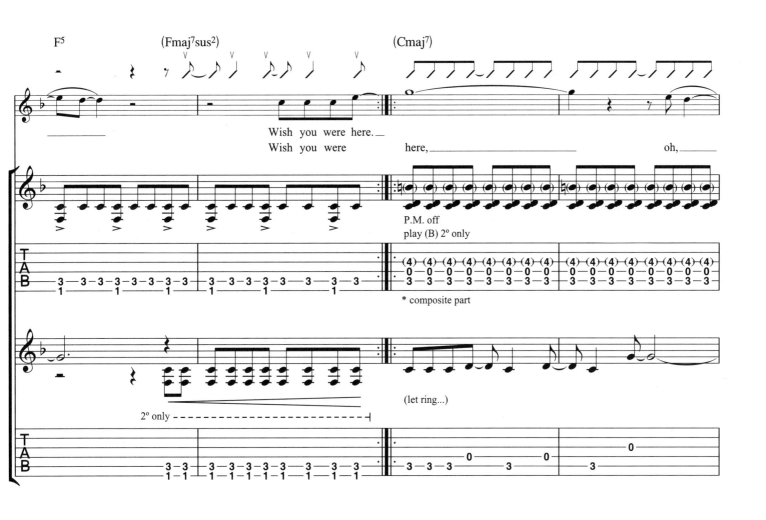

Wish you were here.
Wish you were   here,   oh,

P.M. off
play (B) 2° only

* composite part

(let ring...)

2° only

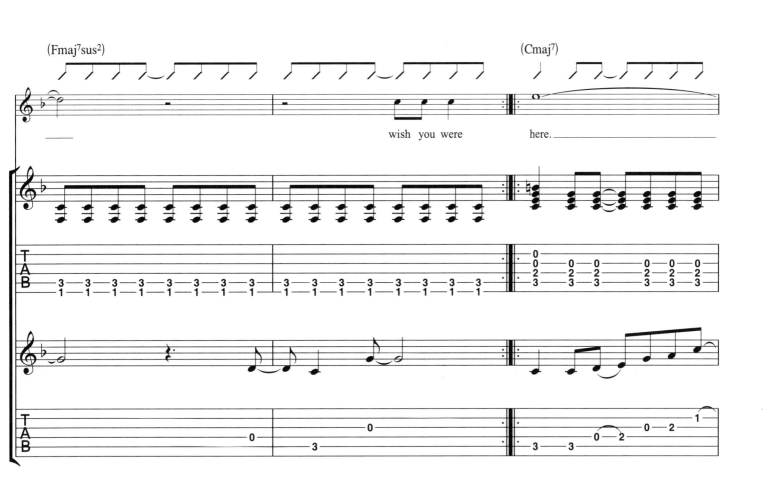

wish you were   here.

65

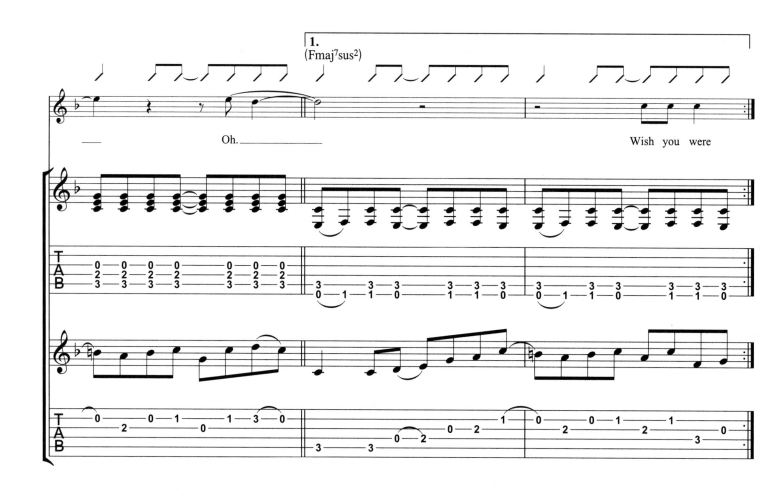

Oh._____   Wish you were

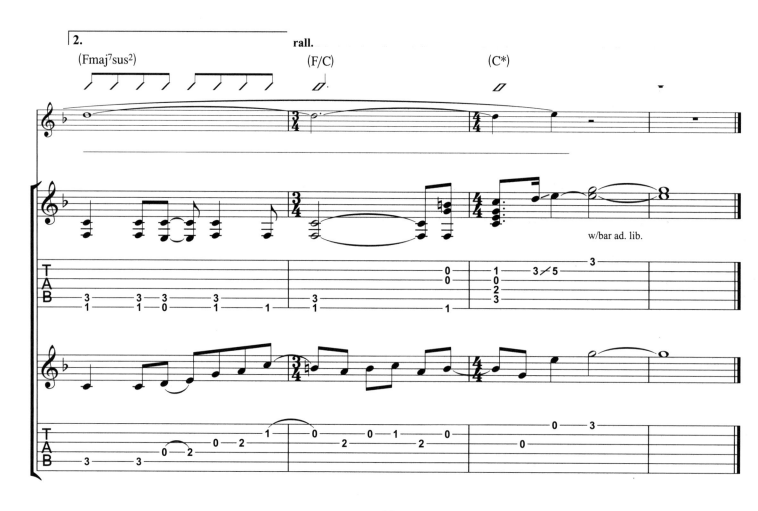

w/bar ad. lib.

66

ROCK N ROLL

Words & Music by Ryan Adams

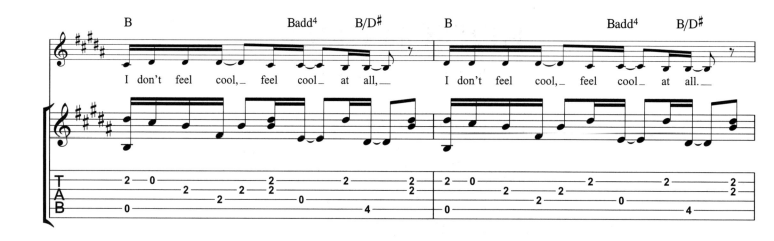

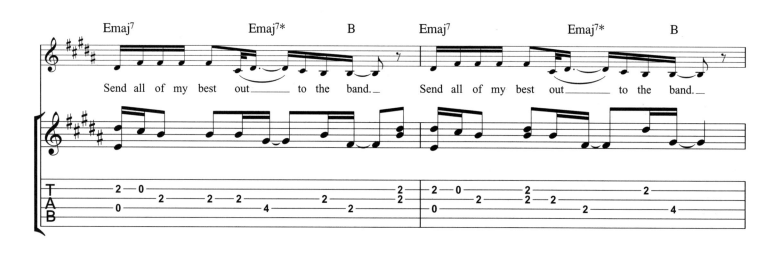

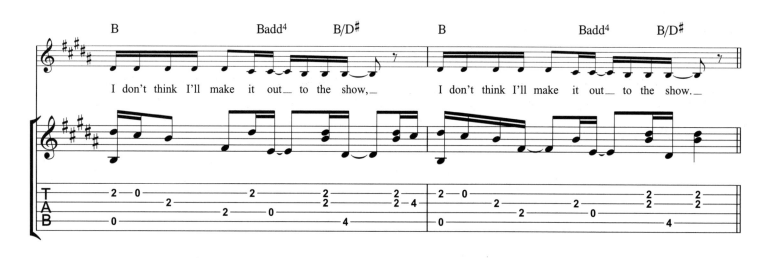

Chorus

ANYBODY WANNA TAKE ME HOME

Words & Music by Ryan Adams

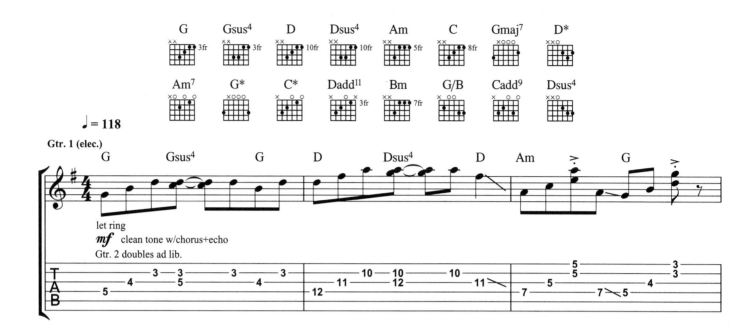

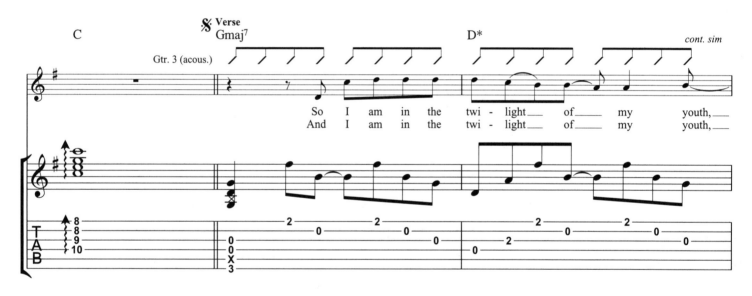

So I am in the twi - light___ of___ my youth,___
And I am in the twi - light___ of___ my youth,___

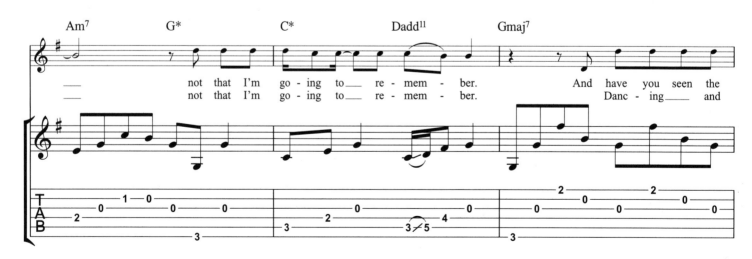

not that I'm go - ing to___ re - mem - ber. And have you seen the
not that I'm go - ing to___ re - mem - ber. Danc - ing___ and

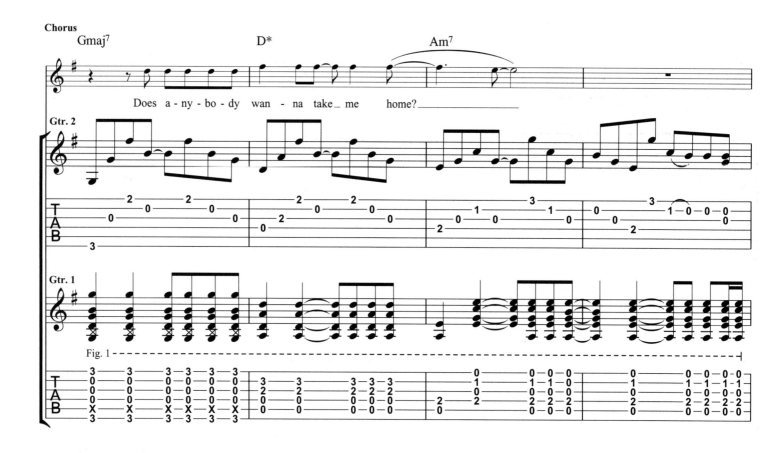

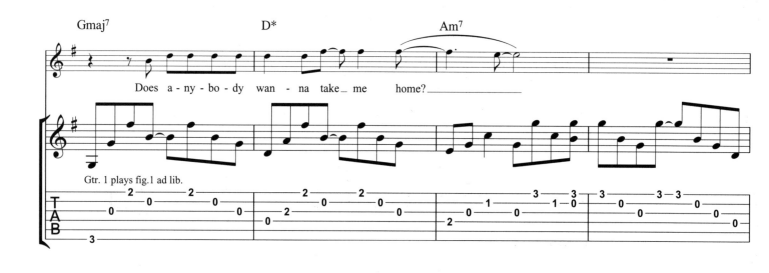

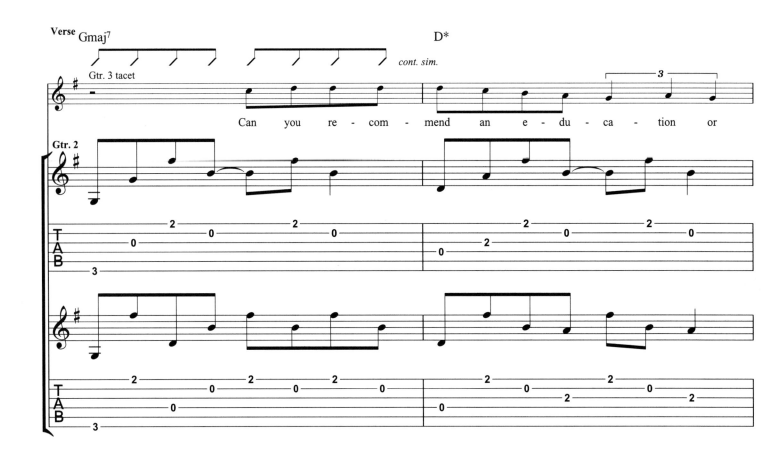

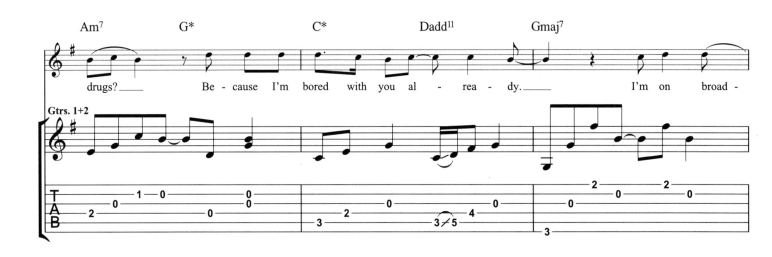

74

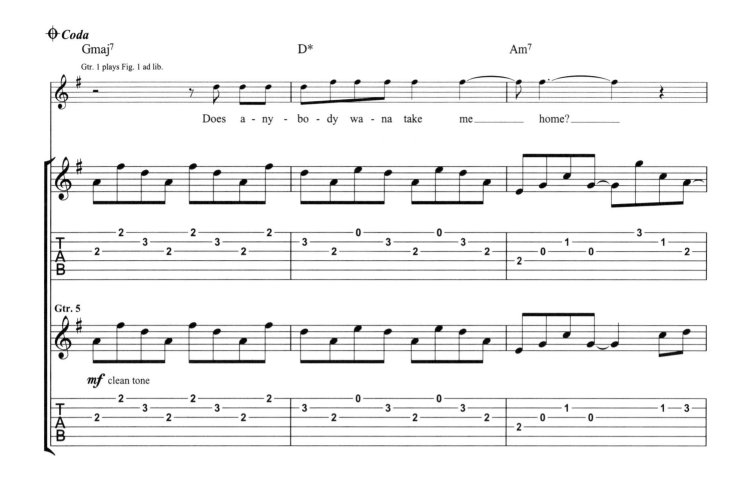

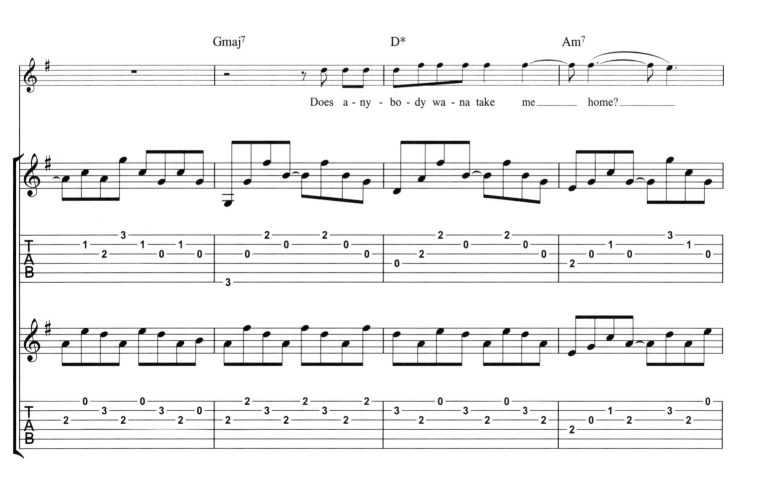

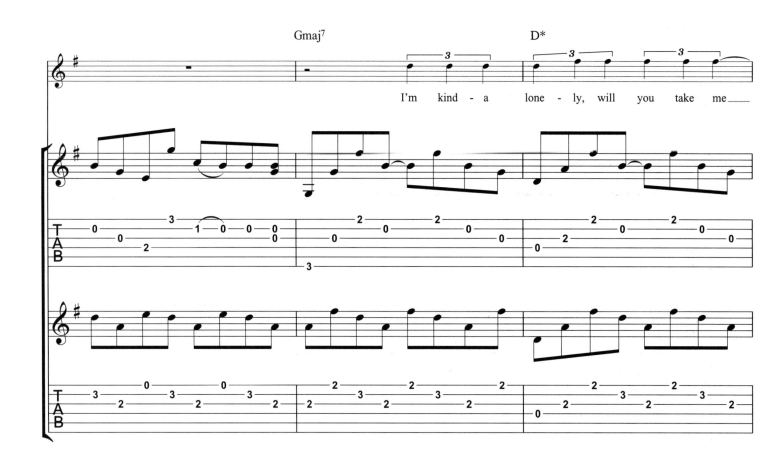

I'm kind - a lone - ly, will you take me___

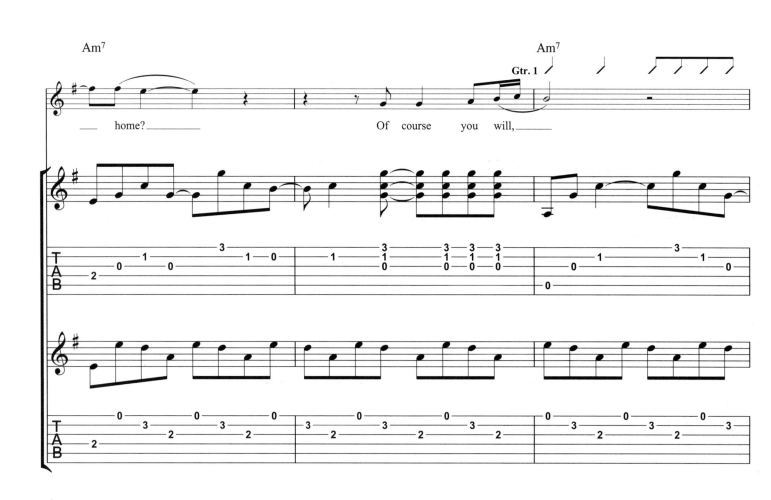

___ home?___ Of course you will,___

of course   you   won't.___   Of course   I'm   crass,___

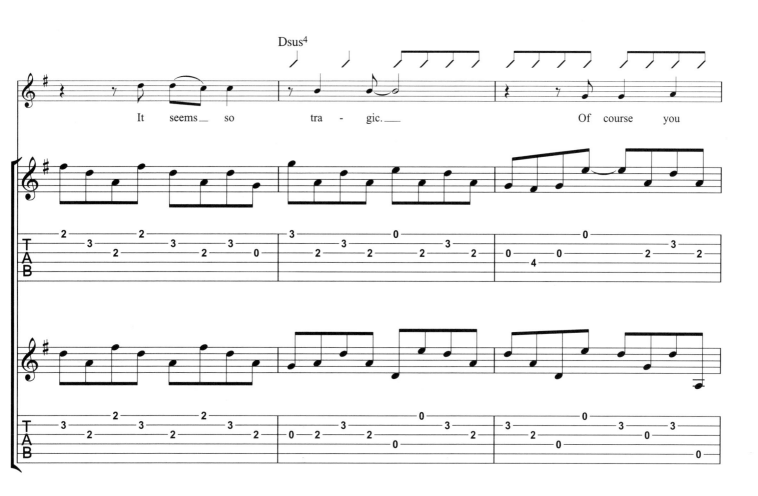

It   seems___   so   tra -   gic.___   Of course   you

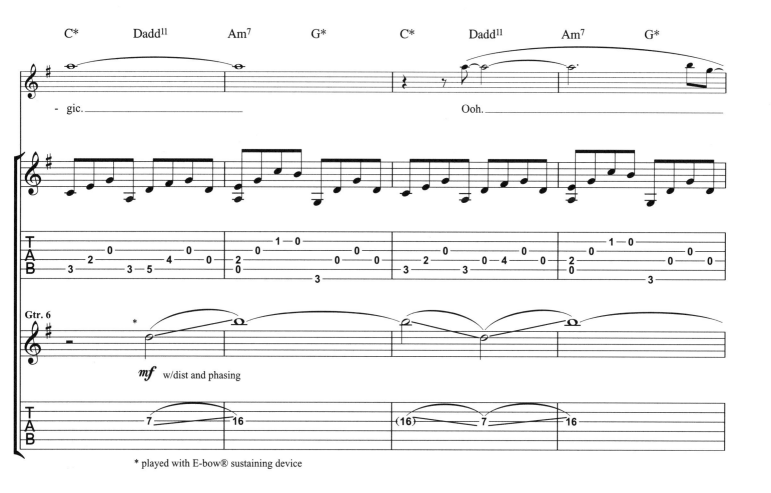

* played with E-bow® sustaining device

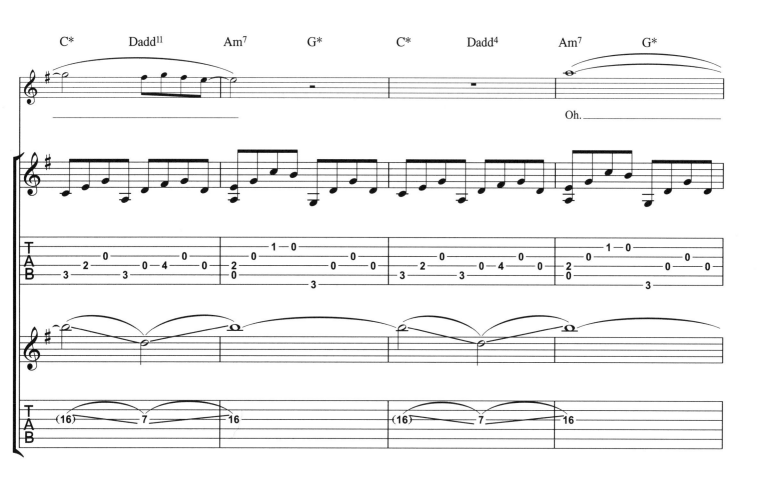

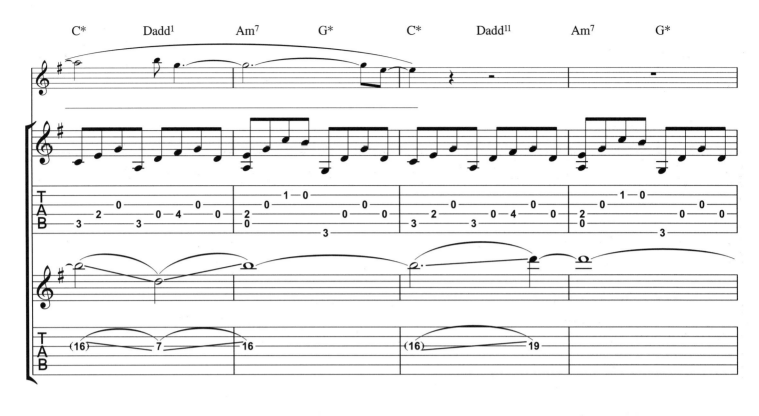

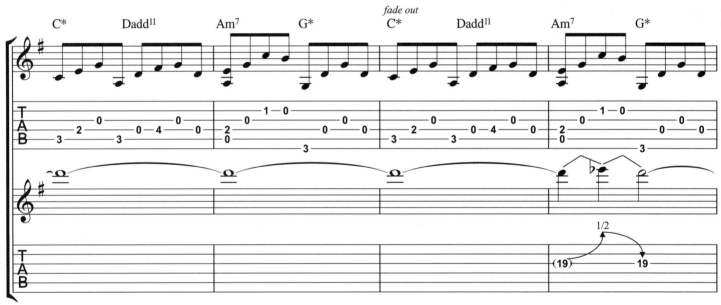

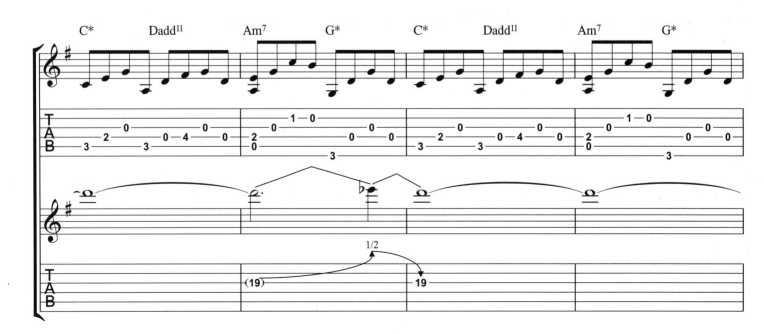

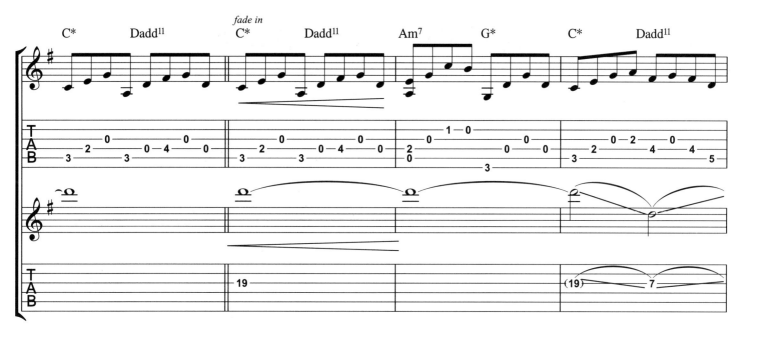

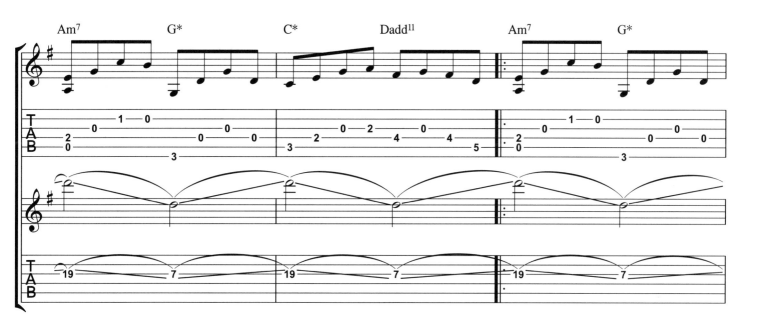

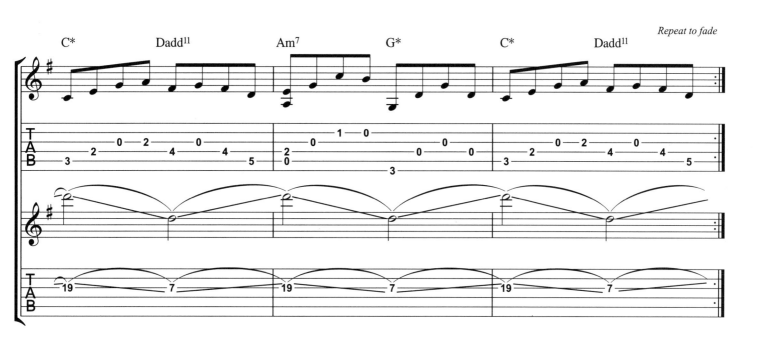

DO MISS AMERICA

Words & Music by Ryan Adams

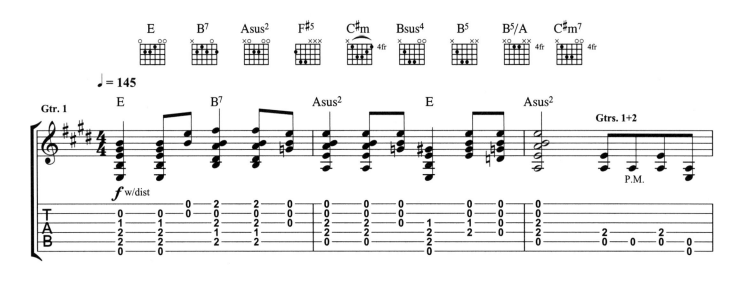

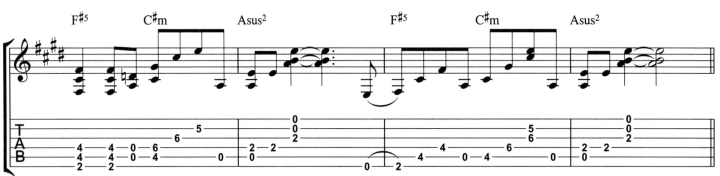

Verse

So tell me, how do you feel with-out your me-di-cine?

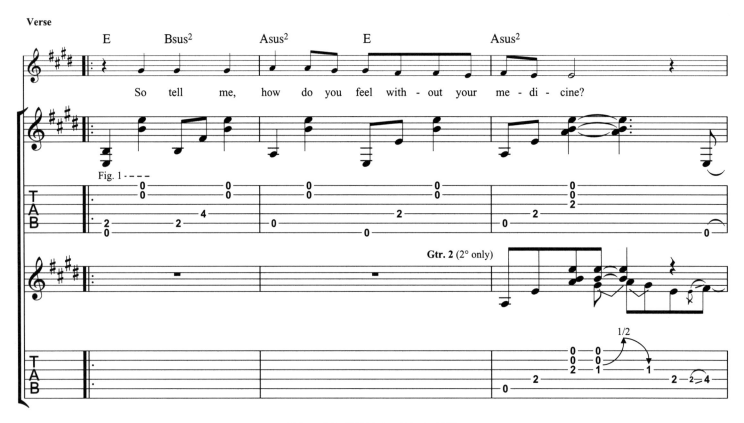

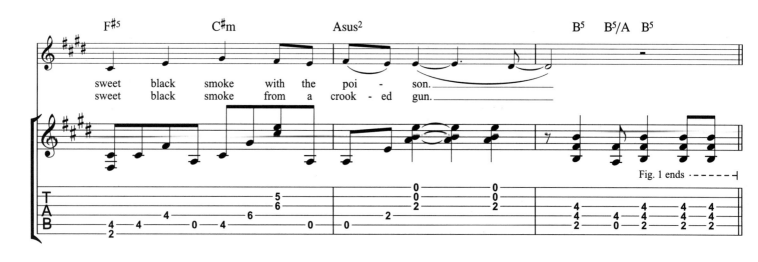

sweet black smoke with the poi - son. _____
sweet black smoke from a crook - ed gun. _____

Fig. 1 ends - - - - - - ⌐

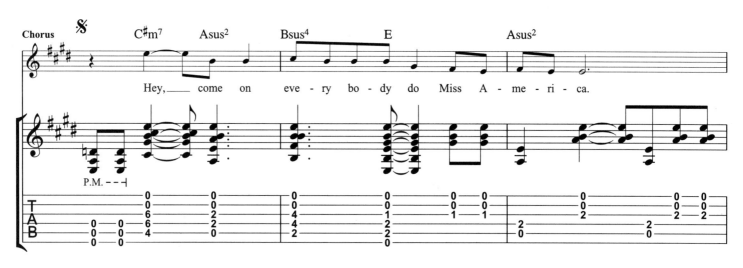

Chorus

Hey, _____ come on eve - ry bo - dy do Miss A - me - ri - ca.

P.M. - - ⌐

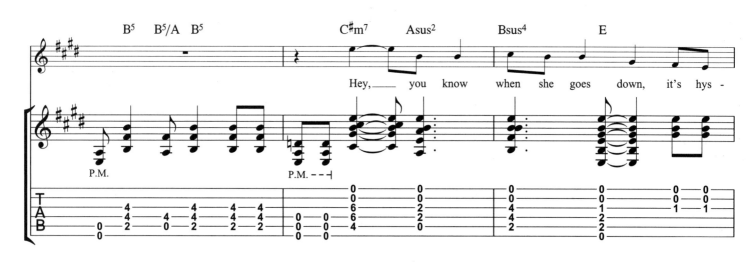

Hey, _____ you know when she goes down, it's hys -

P.M. _____   P.M. - - ⌐

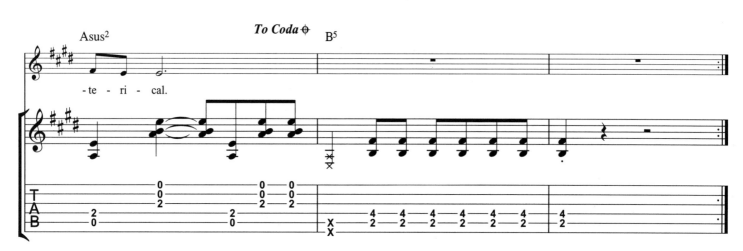

To Coda ⊕

-te - ri - cal.

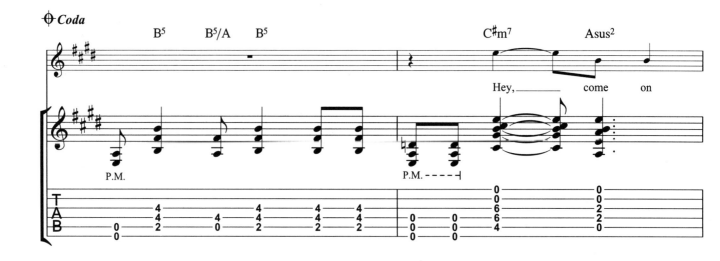

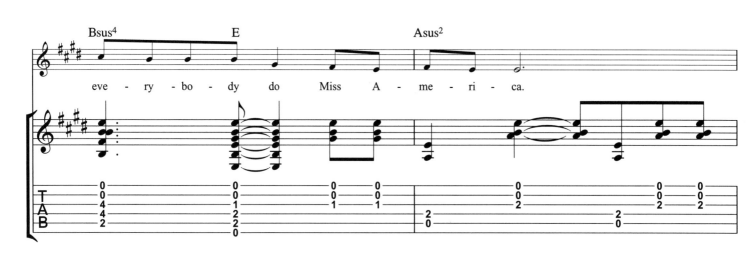

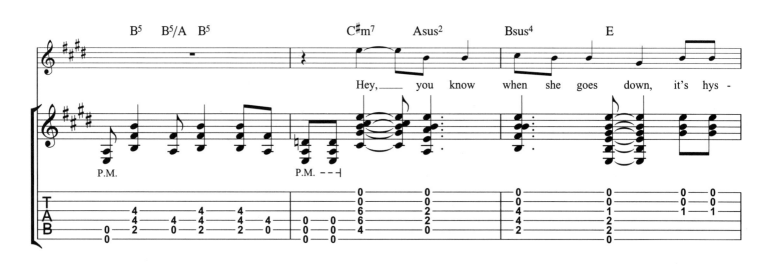

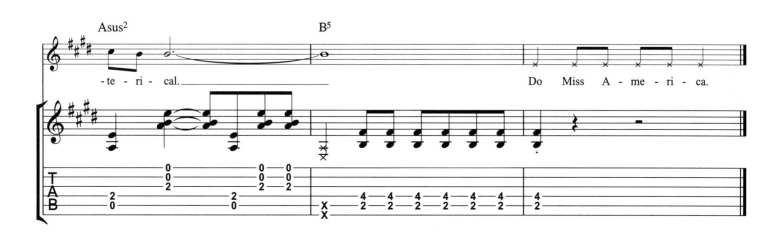

BOYS

Words & Music by Ryan Adams and Johnny T. Yerington

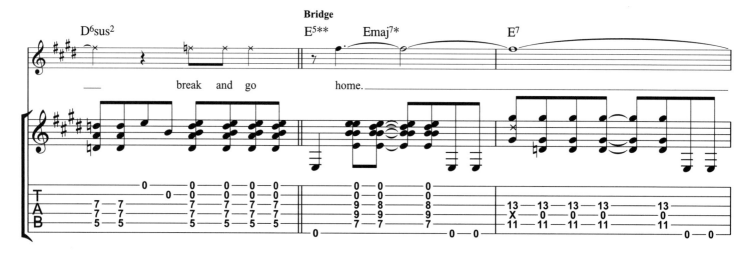

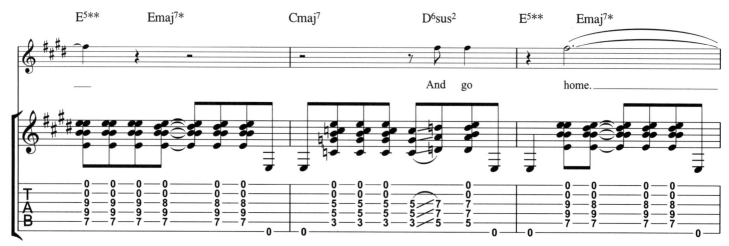

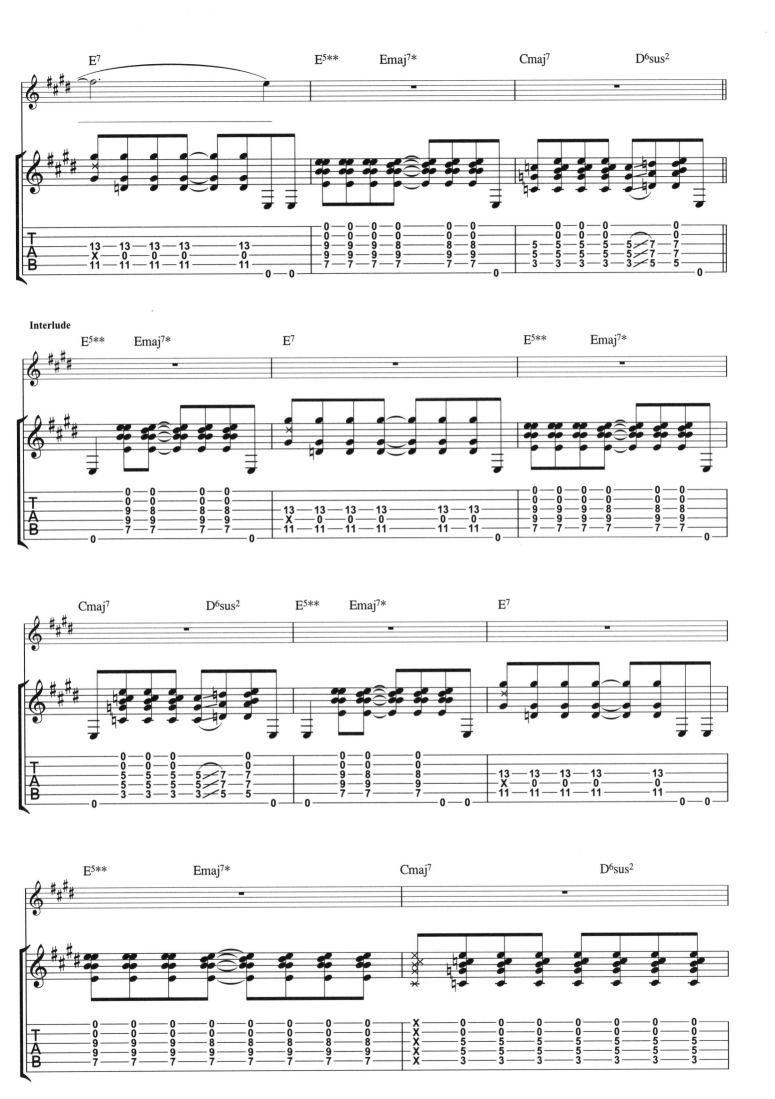

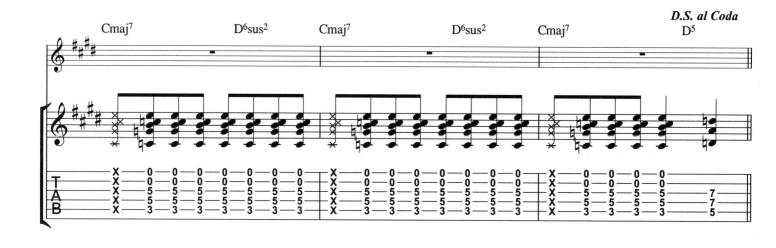

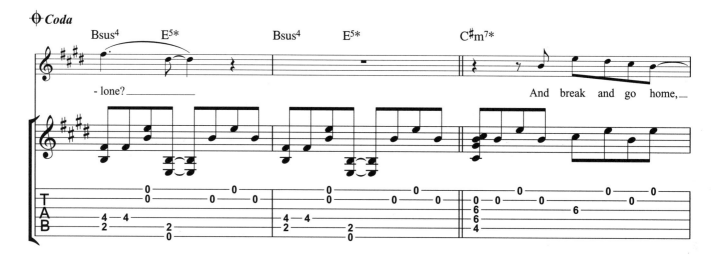

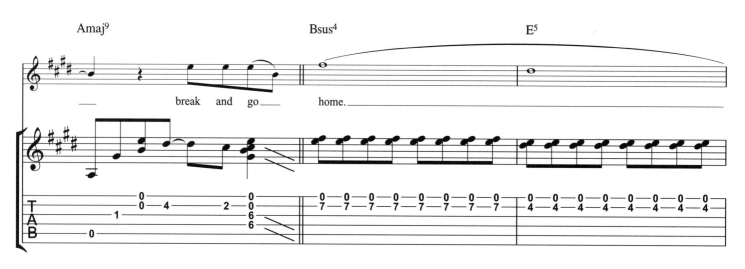

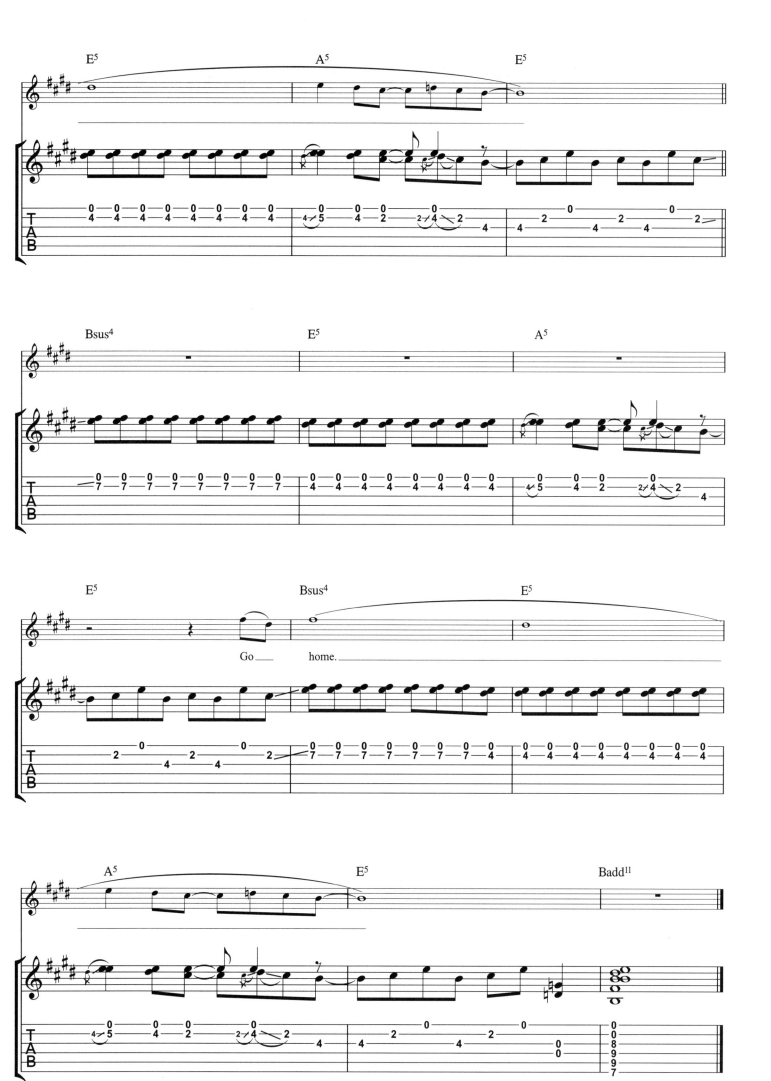

THE DRUGS NOT WORKING

Words & Music by Ryan Adams

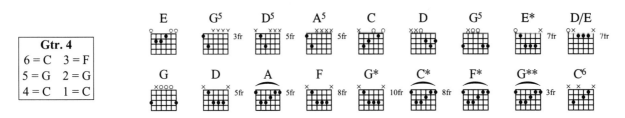

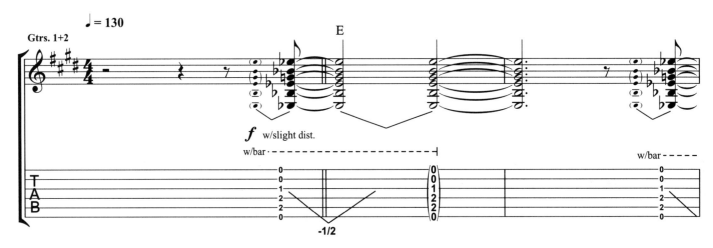

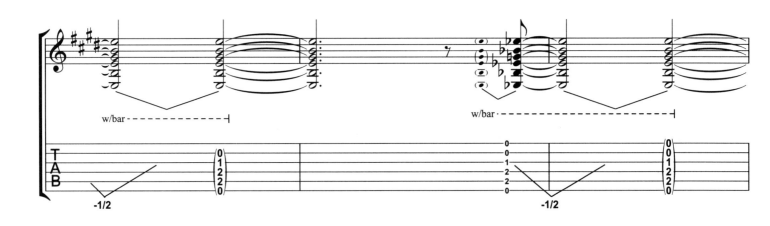

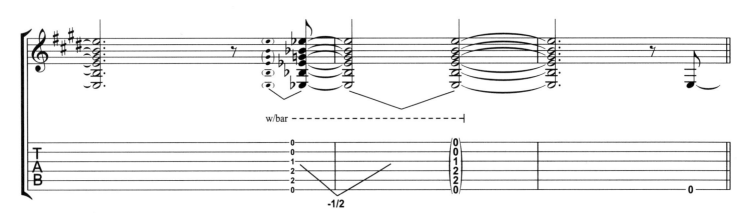

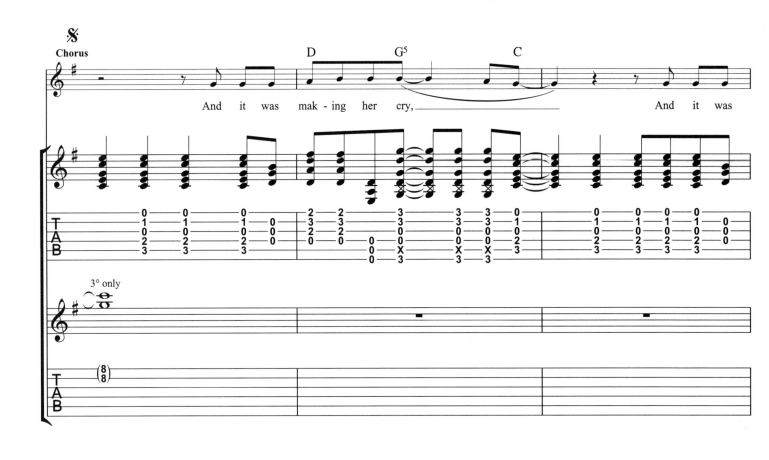

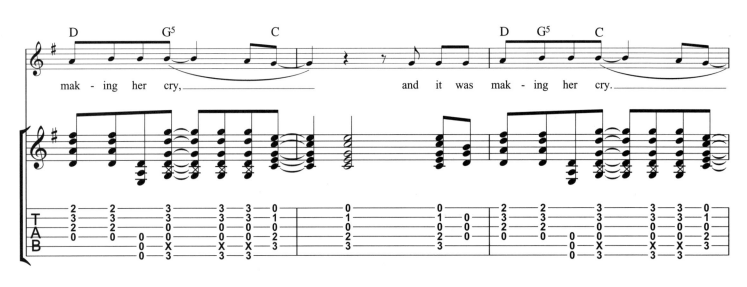

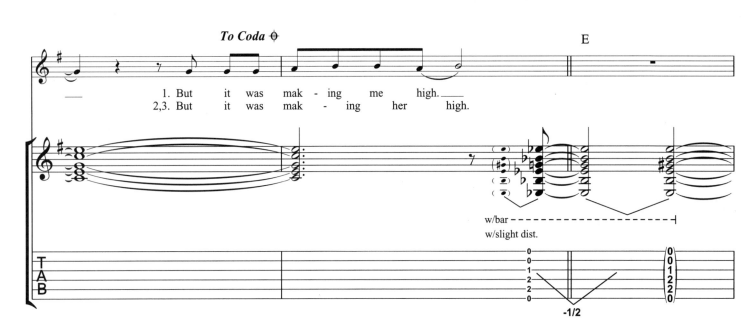

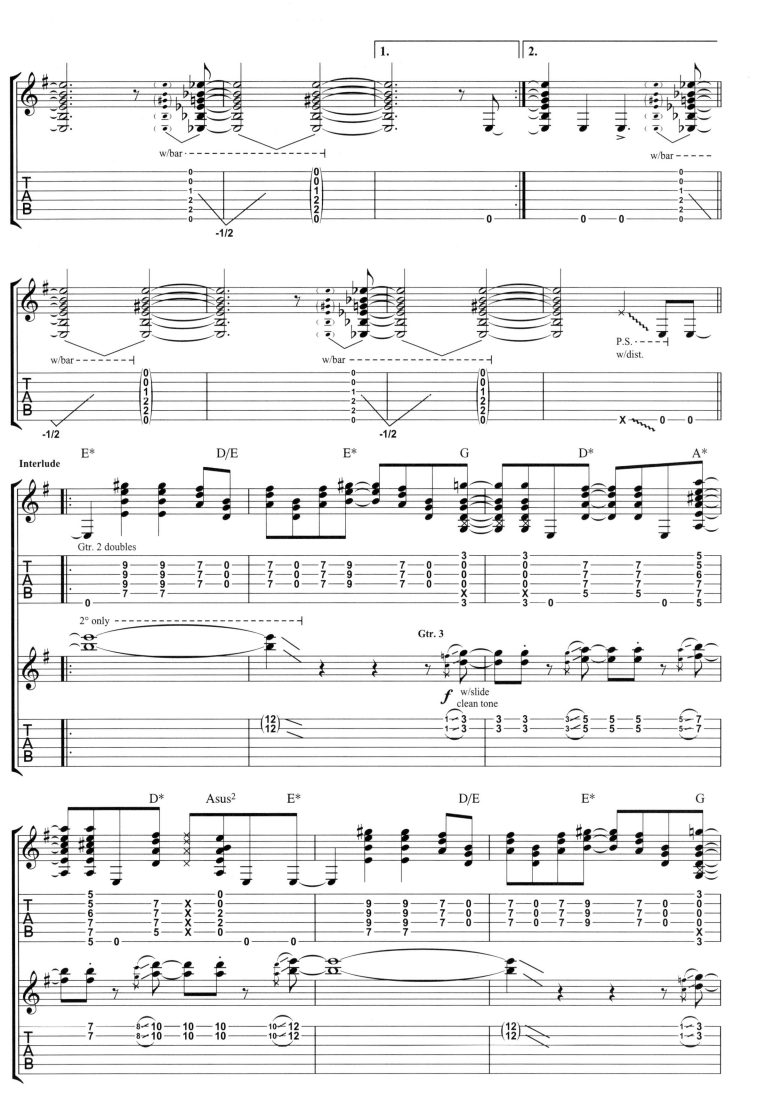

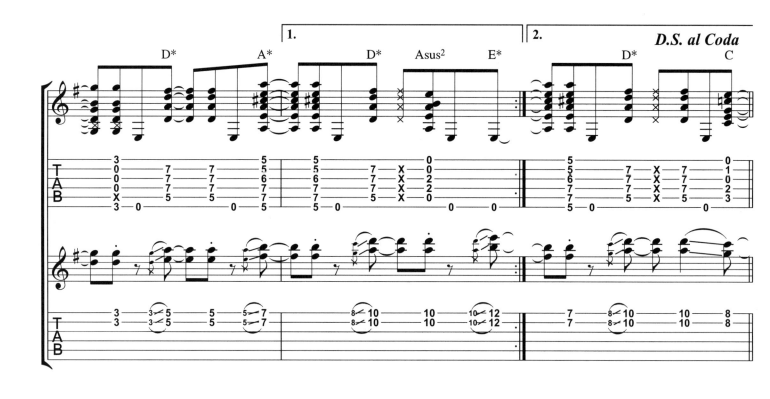

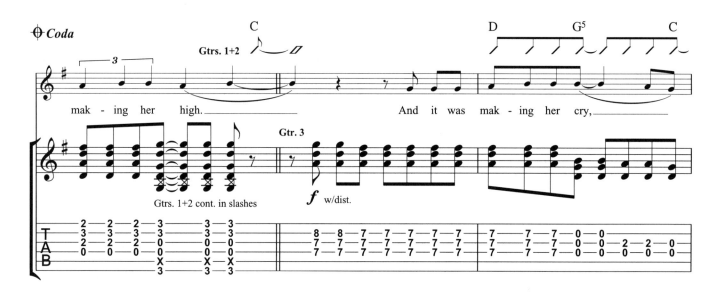

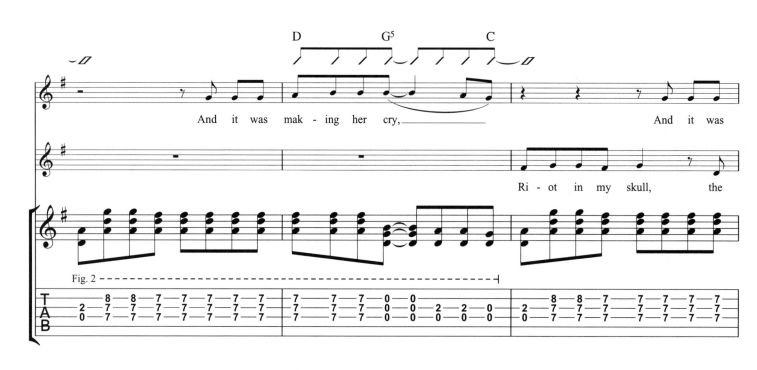

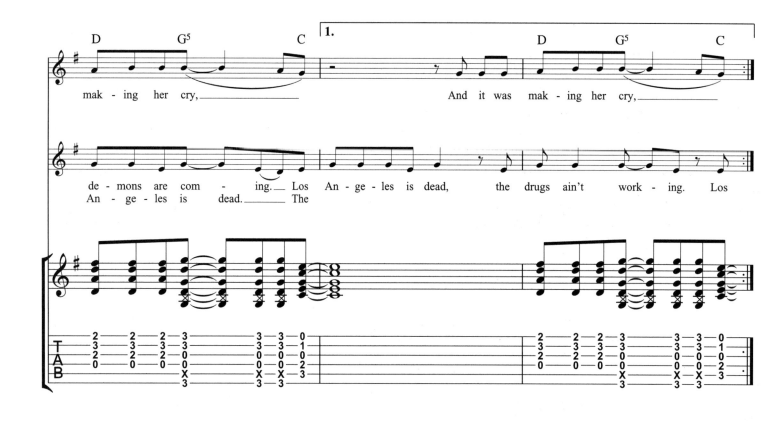

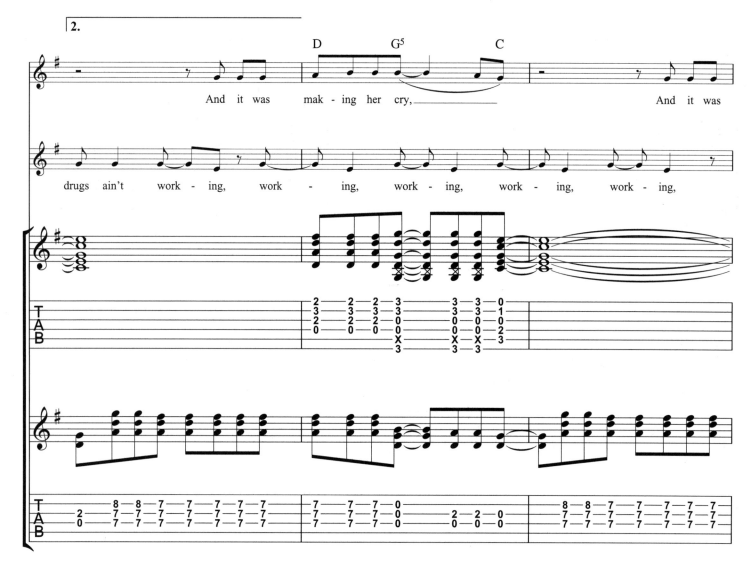

100

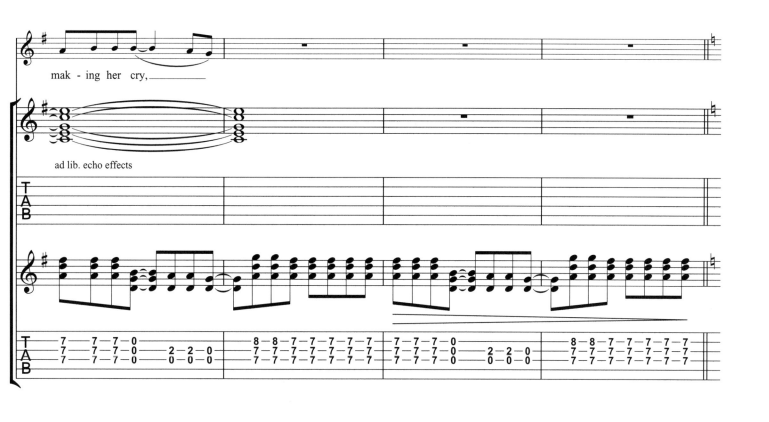

mak - ing her cry,_____

ad lib. echo effects

Keyboards arr. for Gtr.

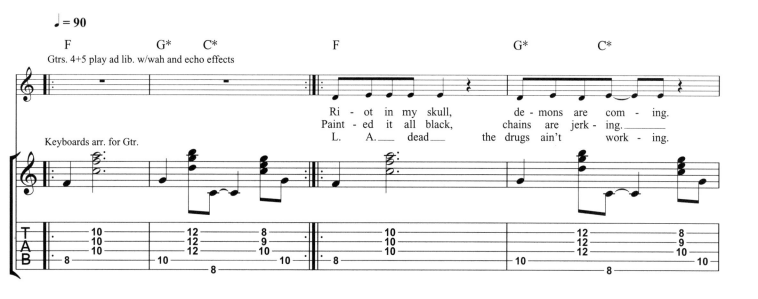

♩ = 90

F   G*   C*   F   G*   C*

Gtrs. 4+5 play ad lib. w/wah and echo effects

Ri - ot in my skull,   de - mons are com - ing.
Paint - ed it all black,   chains are jerk - ing._____
L. A.____ dead____   the drugs ain't   work - ing.

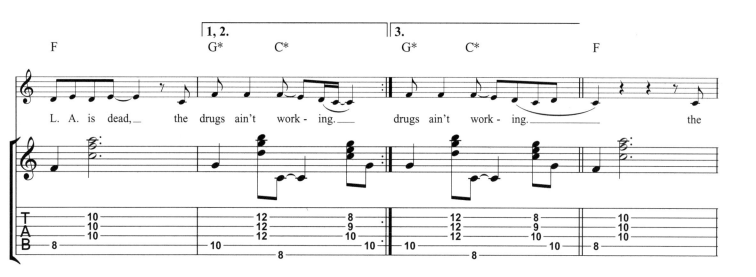

F   G*   C*   G*   C*   F

|1, 2. ||3.

L. A. is dead,____ the drugs ain't work - ing.____   drugs ain't work - ing.____   the

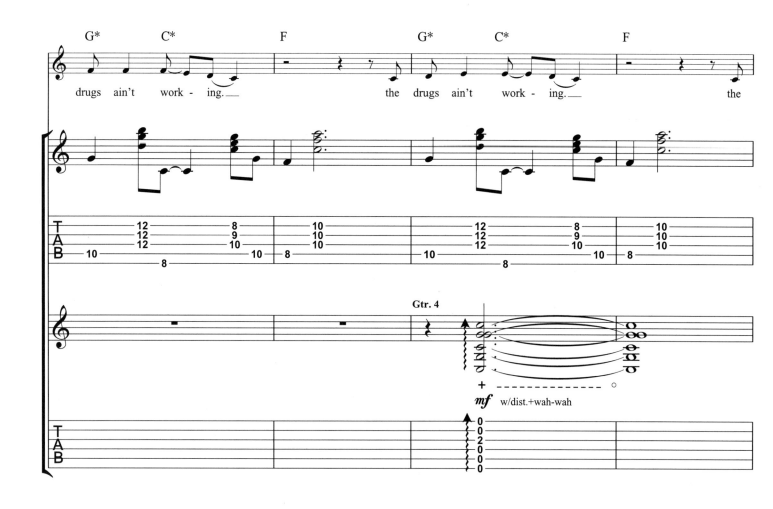

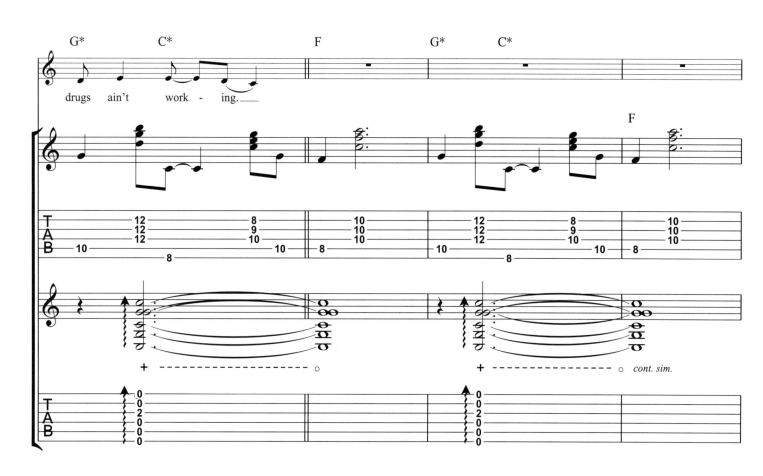

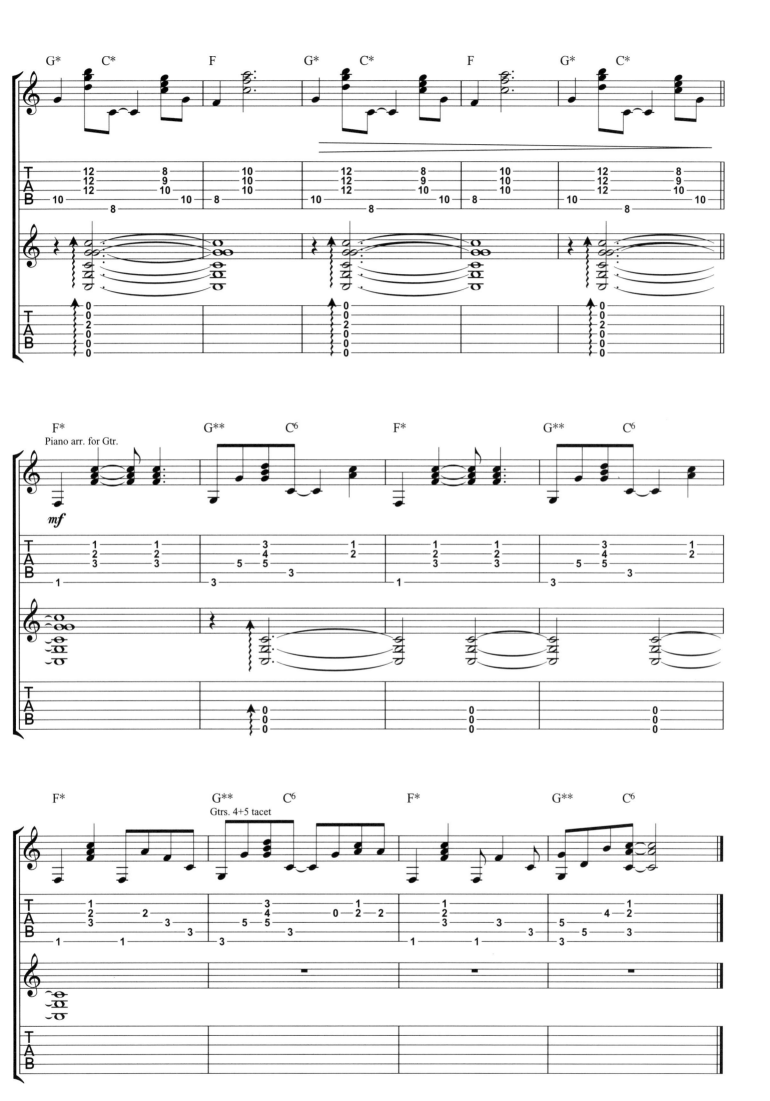

HYPNOTIXED

Words & Music by Ryan Adams

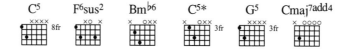

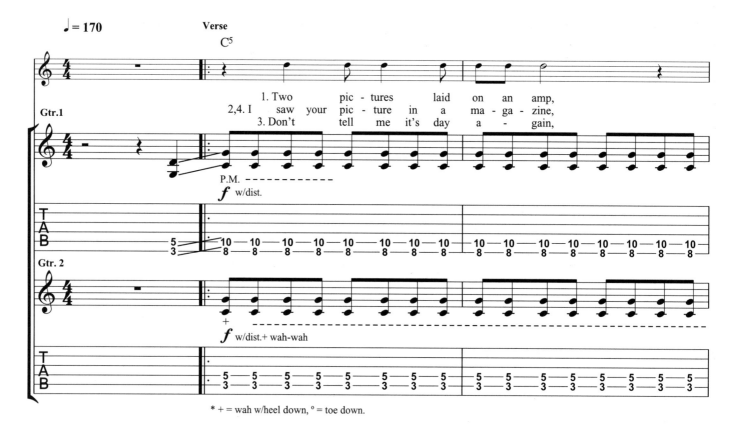

* + = wah w/heel down, ° = toe down.

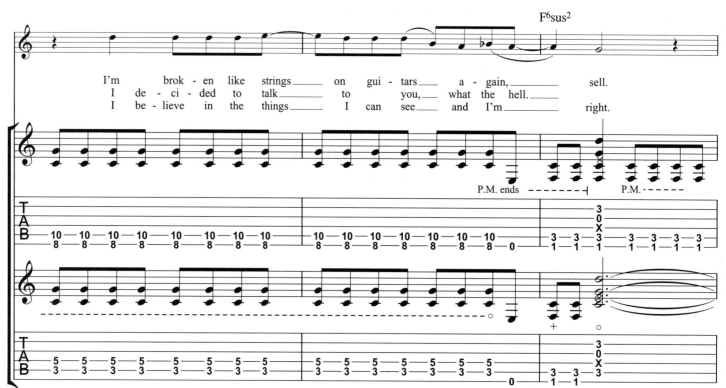

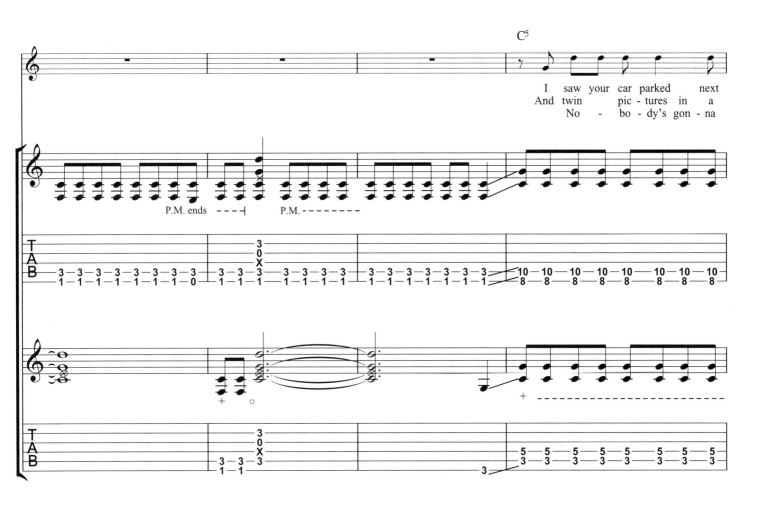

I saw your car parked next
And twin pic - tures in a
No - bo - dy's gon - na

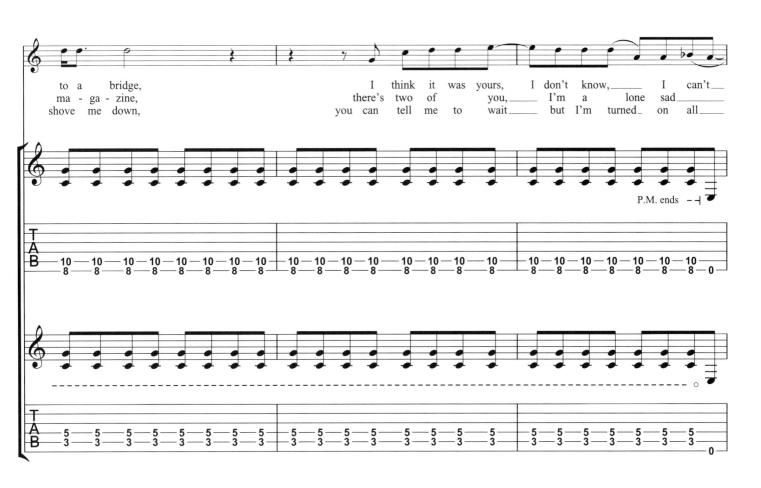

to a bridge,
ma - ga - zine,
shove me down,

I think it was yours, I don't know,_____ I can't
there's two of you,_____ I'm a lone sad
you can tell me to wait_____ but I'm turned_ on all_____

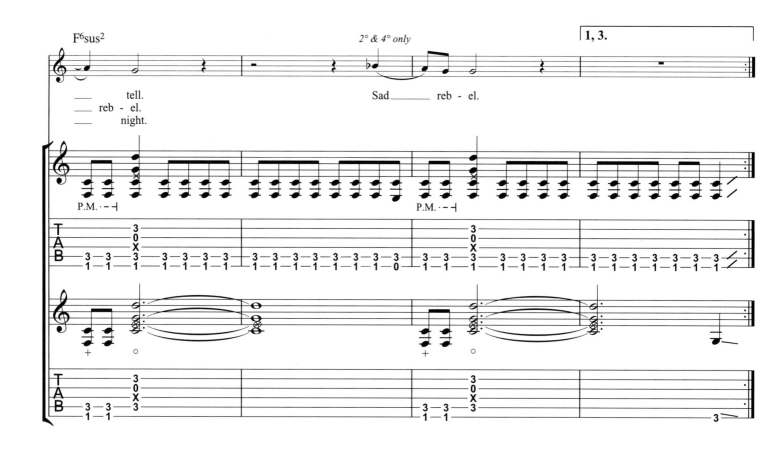

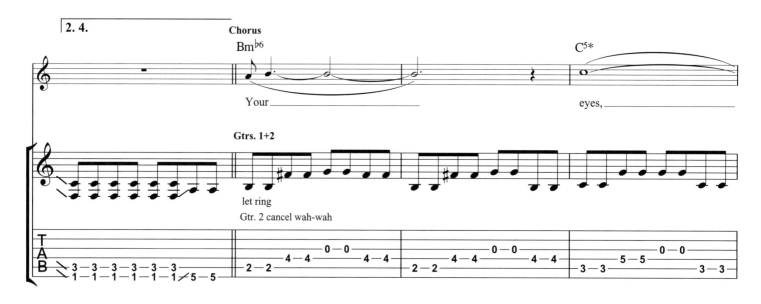

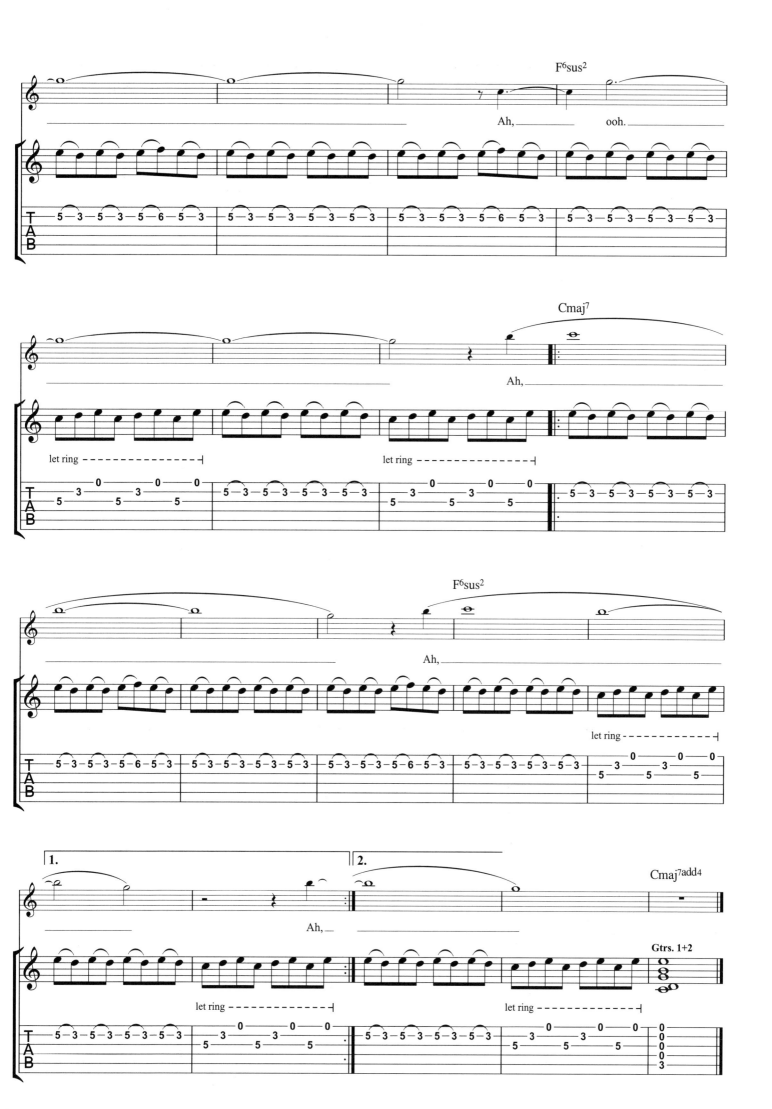

GUITAR TABLATURE EXPLAINED

Guitar music can be notated in three different ways: on a musical stave, in tablature, and in rhythm slashes.

RHYTHM SLASHES are written above the stave. Strum chords in the rhythm indicated. Round noteheads indicate single notes.

THE MUSICAL STAVE shows pitches and rhythms and is divided by lines into bars. Pitches are named after the first seven letters of the alphabet.

TABLATURE graphically represents the guitar fingerboard. Each horizontal line represents a string, and each number represents a fret.

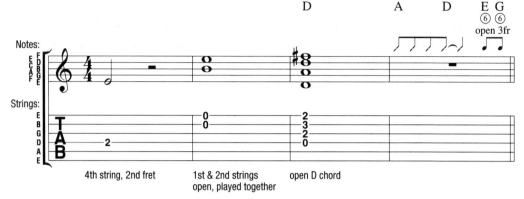

4th string, 2nd fret   1st & 2nd strings open, played together   open D chord

DEFINITIONS FOR SPECIAL GUITAR NOTATION

SEMI-TONE BEND: Strike the note and bend up a semi-tone (1/2 step).

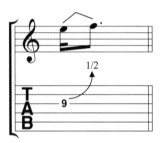

WHOLE-TONE BEND: Strike the note and bend up a whole-tone (whole step).

GRACE NOTE BEND: Strike the note and bend as indicated. Play the first note as quickly as possible.

QUARTER-TONE BEND: Strike the note and bend up a 1/4 step.

BEND & RELEASE: Strike the note and bend up as indicated, then release back to the original note.

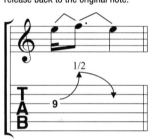

COMPOUND BEND & RELEASE: Strike the note and bend up and down in the rhythm indicated.

PRE-BEND: Bend the note as indicated, then strike it.

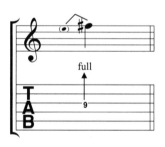

PRE-BEND & RELEASE: Bend the note as indicated. Strike it and release the note back to the original pitch.

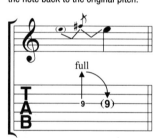

UNISON BEND: Strike the two notes simultaneously and bend the lower note up to the pitch of the higher.

BEND & RESTRIKE: Strike the note and bend as indicated then restrike the string where the symbol occurs.

BEND, HOLD AND RELEASE: Same as bend and release but hold the bend for the duration of the tie.

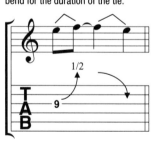

BEND AND TAP: Bend the note as indicated and tap the higher fret while still holding the bend.

VIBRATO: The string is vibrated by rapidly bending and releasing the note with the fretting hand.

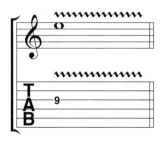

HAMMER-ON: Strike the first note with one finger, then sound the second note (on the same string) with another finger by fretting it without picking.

PULL-OFF: Place both fingers on the notes to be sounded, strike the first note and without picking, pull the finger off to sound the second note.

LEGATO SLIDE (GLISS): Strike the first note and then slide the same fret-hand finger up or down to the second note. The second note is not struck.

SHIFT SLIDE (GLISS & RESTRIKE): Same as legato slide, except the second note is struck.

TRILL: Very rapidly alternate between the notes indicated by continuously hammering on and pulling off.

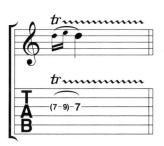

TAPPING: Hammer ("tap") the fret indicated with the pick-hand index or middle finger and pull off to the note fretted by the fret hand.

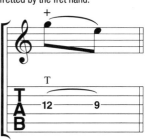

PICK SCRAPE: The edge of the pick is rubbed down (or up) the string, producing a scratchy sound.

MUFFLED STRINGS: A percussive sound is produced by laying the fret hand across the string(s) without depressing, and striking them with the pick hand.

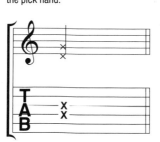

NATURAL HARMONIC: Strike the note while the fret-hand lightly touches the string directly over the fret indicated.

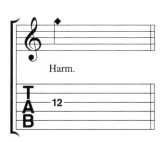

PINCH HARMONIC: The note is fretted normally and a harmonic is produced by adding the edge of the thumb or the tip of the index finger of the pick hand to the normal pick attack.

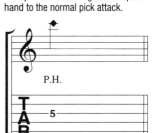

HARP HARMONIC: The note is fretted normally and a harmonic is produced by gently resting the pick hand's index finger directly above the indicated fret (in brackets) while plucking the appropriate string.

PALM MUTING: The note is partially muted by the pick hand lightly touching the string(s) just before the bridge.

RAKE: Drag the pick across the strings indicated with a single motion.

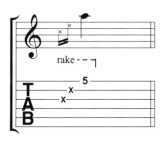

TREMOLO PICKING: The note is picked as rapidly and continuously as possible.

ARPEGGIATE: Play the notes of the chord indicated by quickly rolling them from bottom to top.

SWEEP PICKING: Rhythmic downstroke and/or upstroke motion across the strings.

VIBRATO DIVE BAR AND RETURN: The pitch of the note or chord is dropped a specific number of steps (in rhythm) then returned to the original pitch.

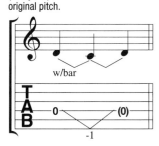

VIBRATO BAR SCOOP: Depress the bar just before striking the note, then quickly release the bar.

VIBRATO BAR DIP: Strike the note and then immediately drop a specific number of steps, then release back to the original pitch.

ADDITIONAL MUSICAL DEFINITIONS

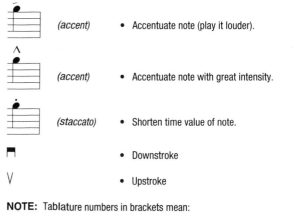 *(accent)*	•	Accentuate note (play it louder).
(accent)	•	Accentuate note with great intensity.
(staccato)	•	Shorten time value of note.
	•	Downstroke
	•	Upstroke

D.%. al Coda

• Go back to the sign (%), then play until the bar marked *To Coda* ⊕ then skip to the section marked ⊕ *Coda*.

D.C. al Fine

• Go back to the beginning of the song and play until the bar marked *Fine*.

tacet

• Instrument is silent (drops out).

• Repeat bars between signs.

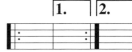

• When a repeated section has different endings, play the first ending only the first time and the second ending only the second time.

NOTE: Tablature numbers in brackets mean:
1. The note is sustained, but a new articulation (such as hammer on or slide) begins.
2. A note may be fretted but not necessarily played.